Penrith Library

		1 7 AUG 2010
3 0 JUL 2005	2 4 APR 2007	3 FEB 2011
- 8 OCT 2005	1 6 MAY 2007	2 1 OCT 2011
	- 2 JUL 2007	
2 2 OCT 2005		
	30/6/08	
23 MAR 2006	/2/09	8 SEP 2011
CIRC Pel		
23 MAY 2006	2 7 AUG 2009 WITHDRAWN	
- 9 JUN 2006	CALReg	
3 1 JUL 2006		
CALReg	1 2 OCT 2009	
	2 9 JAN 2010	
- 5 FEB 2007		

Cumbria

COUNTY COUNCIL

CUMBRIA LIBRARY SERVICES

This book is due to be returned on or before the last date above. It
may be renewed by personal application, post or telephone, if not in
demand.

C.L.18

The
Fireplace
Book

The
Fireplace
Book

An inspirational style guide to the fireplace and its place in the home

Miranda Innes

Thames & Hudson

First published in the United Kingdom in 2000 by
Thames & Hudson Ltd, 181A High Holborn, London WC1V 7QX

Copyright © 2000, Quarto Publishing plc

ISBN 0-500-51004-0

QUAR.FPB

Conceived, designed, and produced by Quarto Publishing plc
The Old Brewery
6 Blundell Street
London
N7 9BH

Manufactured in China by Regent Publishing services, Ltd
Printed in China by Leefung-Asco Printers Ltd

Contents

Introduction

THE NEW BUZZWORD is 'time-poor'. In Western society, everything can be bought – except time. Time is the great leveller, and none of us – rich or poor, captain of industry or harassed single mother – can stretch time or bank it, or successfully demand more. So what the harried go-getter really lacks is quality time. Time just to be. Time, which is not only life enhancing, but life preserving. There are, however, ways to rectify this, from keeping a pet to massages and meditation. But, best, and perhaps easiest, of all, indulge in a real fire.

Trust your own senses. An open fire will make you relax, become more creative, have better relationships, sleep better, and is, in short, the secret of a long and happy life. You may have to work a bit to make one, but the benign warmth and positive glow that a fire radiates can only be bettered by the natural benediction of sunlight. In the winter months, an open fire is a pretty effective sun substitute, and it beats contemplating a radiator.

An open fire is profoundly comforting. It provides a focus, or a stage, around which dogs, cats and people will want to gather, inexorably relaxing into a fluid tumble of interwoven bodies. Once you have succumbed to the seduction of logs and flame, a room without a fire will be a desert. It will have no heart, no life, no centre. And having made your fire, it will take serious inducements to drag you away from it. Suddenly all those games – the chess, the backgammon and the Scrabble – will make sense as a valid excuse to sit by the fireside. Sunday afternoons will be transformed from a temporal wasteland to a precious island of time, littered with journals, magazines, cushions, hot chocolate and all the other messy, cosy fireside paraphernalia.

We are all so hard-pressed that we need an excuse just to sit – offensively called being lazy – and in all the busy melee, are apt to forget what a vital, regenerative function mulling and musing perform. This essential aspect of life is now relegated to sleep, so we look, with the expensive guidance of a therapist, to our dreams to tell us what half an hour by a good fire could reveal. Just letting thoughts quietly rise to the surface in an atmosphere of tranquillity is thoroughly

Above Sixteenth-century gentlemen warm themselves and reflect on the day's events around a large open fire.

Left The warm glow of flames burning brightly in a hearth is enough to make anyone want to curl up on the sofa and relax.

Above A cosy image of a family gathered around the fireside was used to sell a nineteenth-century musical score for the pianoforte.

healing, as anyone who has tried it can attest. If you do not have perennial summer, a river, or whispering trees and a view of mountains to hand, a fire will serve conveniently and leave you just as refreshed.

A fire does much more than simply keep you warm. Certainly a long, cold, damp, dark winter does very little to induce joy and free the positive spirit. An open fire addresses a primitive psychological need, even a spiritual one. A fire is good for the body, the mind and the spirit, and it might just make you a better person. Even if it does not transform you overnight into a soulful and wise elder, you will certainly enjoy the experiment.

Once upon a time, when the icy, dark months of winter set in, there was no alternative to tinder and logs if you did not want to succumb to hypothermia. Or, come the summertime, if you preferred your food cooked rather than raw. Sitting by a blazing fire has always been one of the great pleasures of life, whether impenetrable snow is banked up against the front door or the desert moon is painting the sand dunes blue. It has, however, always been tempered in the past by its associated chores. If a fire is your only form of heat, it is likely that you will look upon it with less than unalloyed affection. The primitive pleasure of a real fire is unfortunately accompanied by the primitive penance of a certain amount of real labour.

But for those of us for whom a fire is an optional extra, when central heating does the serious work of keeping us constantly warm throughout our home, a blazing hearth is quite simply the best nostalgic treat. An open fire is an addictive drug. The labour, when voluntary, is trifling and an essential part of the ritual. Hearth is synonymous with home. Once you have succumbed to the delicious torpor induced by watching the dancing flames punctuated by occasional starbursts of sparks, once you have burned your fingers greedily peeling chestnuts and compared the different sweet aromas of roasting apple and pine, you will find that nothing else quite measures up. At first you may feel that you need an excuse for lighting one, such as Christmas or visiting dignitaries. And then, gradually, insidiously, a proper fire will become one of your comforting essentials.

The fireplace has evolved since smoke and filth were its inevitable companions. Gas-fired fake coals burn just as radiantly as the real thing, cost very little to run, and are wonderfully convenient. They spring instantly and effortlessly into life and die down at your command. Enclosed stoves are cleaner and more economical than an open hearth, and will burn at the rate you ordain, so that you can wake up to the lingering warmth from the night before.

In short, if you are seduced by the notion of a glowing hearth as the heart of your home, you can decide exactly how much effort this will entail, precisely what it will look like, how discreet or dominant it will be, and whether it will be a functional triumph and cook food and heat water and radiators, or just radiate glorious life-enhancing luxury.

Top left A backgammon table that can be drawn close to the fire is an entertaining accompaniment to a relaxing evening in front of the fire.

Bottom left Colourful enamel stoves can be just as cosy as a blazing fire. They emit a steady, constant warmth, and the flames are still visible through the glass door.

Right A wooden stool has been comfortably worn into shape by many a cold visitor to the blazing fire.

The Fascination of Fire

Fire has been venerated since time immemorial, and continues to be a source of pleasure, as well as fear, today. Its many practical uses – as a provider of warmth, light and food – as well as its more luxurious associations, means that there is little chance of man outgrowing either the need or the desire for fire in the near future.

Right A reason why so many people love old houses is often the fantastic fireplaces that come with them.

myths & mystery

Right Crowds of locals and tourists flock to the ancient Sun Temple at Konarak in India; some are intrigued by the building and its history, and others come to pay their religious respects.

FIRE'S GREAT IMPORTANCE to humans as one of life's basic tools, the mystery of its powers, and its seeming capriciousness have made fire divine or sacred to many peoples. Sun-worshipping religions often worship fire as they consider it to be the earthly representative of the sun. The Zoroastrians, for example, show great veneration to fire, and use it in religious ceremonies. However, this religion does not worship fire per se, rather they are representing their god Ahura Mazdah in the form of the pure natural substances that he has created, including water and earth as well as fire.

The belief that fire is sacred is universal in mythology. The Ancient Greeks considered fire to be one of the four basic elements – a substance from which all things were composed – along with water, earth and air. It was the Titan Prometheus who, when Zeus mistreated man by planning to deprive man of fire, smuggled the precious flame from the monopoly of the Gods and gave it to man. The most carefully preserved cult in Rome was that of Vesta, goddess of the hearth. She

Above Sun and fire are often personalised in imagery by flames protruding from a face.

Right With fire came industry, and the firing of stoneware in extremely high-temperature furnaces produced stronger, longer-lasting vessels.

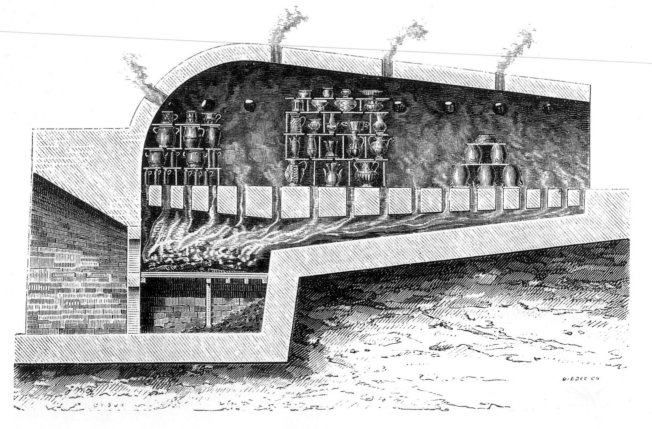

was highly honoured in every household from early times to the beginning of Christianity. Her public cult maintained a sacred building in which her priestesses, the vestal virgins, guarded the holy communal fire and never let it go out.

Fire held the secrets of arcane arts, and Prometheus was worshipped as a god of craftsmen. The discovery of the uses of fire was the catalyst for the arts of metalwork and ceramics and accompanied a huge leap forward for civilisation. Considering its powers in this field alone, it is not surprising that the gods guarded it possessively.

quirky fireplace developments

Left Ornate chimney breasts were the modern art of Renaissance Europe.

Top left Fireside tools come in a wealth of shapes and sizes, but the basic equipment still includes coal scuttle, brush, shovel and poker.

Middle left The invention of matches in the mid-nineteenth century made lighting a fire far less laborious than hitherto.

Bottom left It was hoped that large fireplaces would heat the large expanses of medieval halls, but, unfortunately, they were rarely that effective.

THE CONTAINMENT AND control of fire has developed over the centuries. The woodcutter was a vital, overworked creature who was responsible for the warmth, food and scant comfort of medieval times and before. Wood, peat, twigs and dried dung were the only sources of fuel, and lighting a fire, as well as tending it to ensure it stayed alight, was a time-consuming business. Until the invention of matches in the mid-nineteenth century, it is likely that the flints or steel that provided the initial spark were kept close to hand. Tinder consisted of bark, dried leaves, twigs, bracken and other plant material, such as the papery husks from birch trunks – also known as punk.

When fires were such a troublesome business they were not abundant. As many as possible would warm their frozen fingers at the single source of heat in the great hall, and very likely slept close by too. Elsewhere, a primitive form of central heating was often afforded by keeping livestock at one end of a house, and having a fire at the other. When dwellings progressed from a single room and storey to several, with fireplaces on each floor above each other and back to back, the complicated matter of effective flues had to be tackled, and the chimney breast became one of the structural elements in a house. In Europe, until the Reformation, a Papal chimney tax contributed to a general reluctance to build chimneys, but after 1529 there was an increase in intricately patterned brick chimneys and ornate fireplaces depicting Biblical scenes, hunting and an assortment of deities. Plaster had advantages that the sixteenth-century artisan was quick to grasp – a mould could be made and used repeatedly, and the material itself was relatively cheap and easy to come by. It is likely that a plasterer would have had a pattern book from which his clients could select designs.

Above Woodcutters would make good use of a portion of the wood they gathered each day to warm their humble forest dwellings at night.

The increasing proliferation of fireplaces in the home may have brought a degree of comfort, but warmth, particularly in crowded timber buildings, has its attendant dangers – the Great Fire of London in 1666 wiped out much of the city. But this disaster was turned to good advantage, and the city was rebuilt, largely of stone, with wider streets. The new city became the capital of the commercial world, knocking Antwerp off its perch, and heralded a period of prosperity.

Boston too had its fair share of city fires. In New England, fireplaces were huge and profligate with timber. Gradually, they were refined and designed to work more efficiently. Nevertheless, there was, among the Puritan community, a general fear that being too warm within would weaken the constitution and make one all the more vulnerable to the cold. While churches made it a point of principle to have neither heat nor light, taverns boasted the attractions of copious alcohol and blazing fires. It can hardly have been a surprise that many hardworking men eschewed religion, preferring the convivial comforts of the alehouse.

One element of the fireplace that has seen little change since medieval times is the traditional fireside tools. All those black, forged-iron tongs and pokers, shovels, andirons and grates would be the only twentieth-century tools that a medieval time-traveller would feel at home with. He would be mystified by the simple magic of matches and paper, let alone the cheat's repertoire of gas, firelighters and paraffin.

Above In 1666, 87 churches and 13,000 homes in the City of London were destroyed by a fire that started in a baker's shop.

simple pleasures

Right The fire is the central feature in this historical cartoon of a medieval kitchen. All the contemporary cooking paraphernalia is evident, from bellows to griddles and spits.

FIRE WAS THE original source of heat, light and food. Today these three central needs are met with devices far more technologically advanced than fire, yet this element is still extremely popular for the cooking of food. Certain foods, such as roast chestnuts or joints of pork, were and still are delicious when cooked among the coals or barbecued in the heat from an open fire. Good kitchen shops sell chestnut roasters that look like perforated frying pans. It is advisable to make a cut in each chestnut before sitting them over hot coals, to avoid explosions – peeling and eating them combines pleasure and pain in equal measure. Although spits are not common household items, hog roasts are still popular social events in towns and villages. In a watered down form, families enjoy barbecues on warm summer evenings. Anything that can be cooked on a barbecue can be cooked on an open fire, and in Spain, cast-iron trivets and black, iron paella pans are still standard fireside accessories, and whole heads of garlic may well be roasted among the coals. Grilled vegetables marinated with olive oil, garlic and herbs are fashionable, healthy and delicious, and behave impeccably over an open fire.

In times past, over the fire the iron cauldron would hang on a chain, familiar from tales of witches. Cooking paraphernalia at its most sophisticated would have consisted of the blackened pot, a spit, a griddle, a trivet and a kettle, while on the sides of the fireplace may be narrow shelves that operated as ovens. Further above the flames may have been a joint of pork or a bundle of fish, being 'smoked'. Smoking was one of the few ways to preserve food – wood smoke contains tar products that preserve the meat, and particular flavours can be imparted by the use of different woods. The duration of the process could vary from several hours to several days, and the most commonly used woods were, and are, beech, hickory, oak and chestnut. In those conditions cooking was a matter of observation and experience, and there were no handy controls to reduce the heat to simmer, or raise it to sear. Similarly today, the indoor open grills that are available tend to be unpredictable and therefore experimental, but the fun of watching, turning, and tasting is immense.

fireplaces
as
art

THROUGHOUT HISTORY, THE designers of the finest homes have not only given the fireplace a functional purpose but have also made it a decorative point of interest. Over the centuries, rooms of any importance have been provided with fireplaces, and within living memory many houses would have been uninhabitable without them. Although supplanted by central heating in the last few decades, the open fire has been a consistent architectural feature of homes in America, Europe and Australia ever since there have been solid structures in these countries, and is no less popular now that it is no longer necessary. The multitude of fireplace designs and styles through the ages reflect the various fashions and developments in technology alongside the depleting natural resources and changing social attitudes.

As the world became more travelled, features of the fashionable fireplace and decorative whims spread from country to country, widening the variety of styles that were available. The Renaissance in fourteenth-century Italy was a particularly rich time in the field of design and creative development. Under the powerful patronage of the Este, Medici, Gonzaga, Visconti, and Sforza families the arts, including architecture, lurched forward. If you were in a

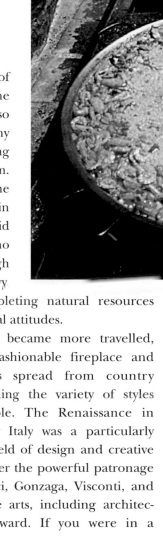

Above A festival in Spain incorporates a paella competition, where vast pans of paella are cooked above huge fire-pits.

Left The engraving that decorated many a Tudor fireplace is reproduced today for admirers of historical design.

Left The Etruscan
motifs clearly date this
fireplace to the late
eighteenth century.

position to commission Leonardo da Vinci to design your party costumes, as was Ludovico il Moro, you did not stint on architects. This was also the time of poetic conceits and clever paradoxes, when everything, from the humblest trinket box to the grandest ballroom, was covered with decorative devices. Every aspect of life from interior decor to doublet and hose was covered in symbols, the equivalent of the designers' initials to be found on T-shirts and smart luggage today. Fireplaces were no exception, and carried their owner's credentials in symbolic form.

The Spaniard Balthasar Gracian described Italian Renaissance conversation thus: 'Emblems, hieroglyphs, fables, and mottoes are as precious stones in the gold of elegant discourse', and so it was with fireplaces. A Renaissance family could not settle down comfortably by the fire unless it was embellished with a frieze of prancing putti, carved and gilded mouldings, heraldic eagles, swags, ribbons, pilasters and dentil edgings. Such fireplaces couldn't fail to make a grandiose architectural statement in their own right as straightforward decoration, whether lit or swept. From this time onward, fireplace design never really looked back. That is not to say that it continued to be as dramatic or decorative as

Above Massive sculptures adorn the sides of the carved chimney breast in the ostentatious manner so beloved by Renaissance Italy.

Left This unique, colorful, complicated Russian fireplace depicts a folk story.

Above The Italians were so fanatical about art that their talents even spread to the chimney pots, which have been designed to resemble miniature houses.

during the Renaissance, but the fireplace has continued to receive much attention by architects and designers ever since.

Contemporary fireplace designers, faced with competition from central heating, have reached a similar conclusion to that reached by Renaissance architects, that the hearth must look good summer or winter, but their means are very different. Where the Renaissance was all about flaunting your wealth and power, with massive beetling fireplaces to indicate status, today smart fireplaces can be small and sleek or large and bold, but whichever it is they invariably look good.

The artistic accomplishments of a fireplace do not have to stop at its design; rather it can be extended past this to the embellishment of the mantle. The Victorians perfected this art, and took it to extremes. But the personal touch of using the mantle as a gallery for flowers, treasured possessions and objets d'art can bring a touch of originality to the plainest fireplace.

a family focus

THE LATIN WORD 'focus' means fire or hearth, and in its contemporary sense conveys its fundamental and continuing importance – fireplaces are, and always have been, the heart and centre of a home. For centuries, fireplaces have been a place for family, friends and laughter as well as a place of intimacy and privacy.

Although we no longer depend on fire alone to provide warmth, behind closed doors we continue to defy the hostile elements outside by curling up beside the fire. Such an atmosphere makes the area around the fireplace the perfect place for a family gathering – as the fire soothes the minds of all present, thus cancelling out any sibling rivalries or petty squabbles among family members. Fireplaces bring to everyone not only a feeling of warmth and relaxation, but by appealing to all our senses, a feeling of being down to earth – a part of nature.

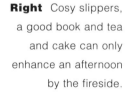

Right Cosy slippers, a good book and tea and cake can only enhance an afternoon by the fireside.

Left This historical painting shows a mother and her children, as well as the rest of the family and local community, making good use of the warmth emitted from the cooking fire.

Fireplaces of the World

From the most humble and ephemeral Rajasthan mud house, to the grandest Roman palazzo, fires and fireplaces are a significant part of life and architecture. In the hotter, poorer corners of the world, fires in the open, even if they are only recycled oil cans with a hole in the base, are the principle means of cooking. However, wherever a home has any degree of permanence, there is a fireplace.

Right A Somalian man watches over the flames in his outdoor bread oven. For him, fire is the only way of turning ingredients into something edible – electricity is not an option.

Asia & Africa

IN PARTS OF India, the women decorate the wall around the fire with elaborate papier-mâché fretwork, twinkling with tiny mirrors, relief patterns and delicate chevron edges moulded by hand from a mixture of paper pulp and clay, and then painted white. In Africa, the Ndebele create a similar structure, using egg boxes and cardboard, and incorporating any decorative objects that come to hand, such as junked chrome hubcaps. The whole piece is then painted in a jazzy geometry of bright colours, like a psychedelic Paul Klee painting.

In central China, where the difference between summer and winter temperatures is huge, the traditional buildings are made of mud, which is not only freely available, but also perfect for its insulating properties. These are known as 'one light, two dark' buildings, and consist of three rooms facing south, with a tiled roof extending to wide, overhanging eaves that shield the inhabitants from the fierce glare of the high summer sun. The rooms are also warmed in winter, when the sun is a precious commodity and low in the sky. The central room is open to light and air, and at the back there is a plinth extending sideways into the enclosed rooms on each side. A fire is lit beneath this in winter, and the warmth is channelled into the two darker rooms, making a primitive but effective heated platform upon which the inhabitants sleep. Much of Japan endures winter muffled by deep snow, and a blazing open fire is traditionally sunk into the floor, providing a form of underfloor heating, and surrounded by tatami mats. Cooking often takes place in iron or steel cauldrons over the blazing flames.

Top left An African woman has her hands full tending her young child while kneading bread in a large clay dish over the flames of her simple oven.

Bottom left Above a central sunken fire in a traditional Japanese room hangs a kettle from a bamboo pole. A blackened bamboo fish brings a single touch of decoration to the room.

Right In warm climates and poor countries, outside fires are common. Here, a Kashmiri prepares a large pot of food on a pile of smoking logs.

southern Europe

IN SPAIN, PORTUGAL, Greece and Italy, fireplaces are a winter necessity. Peasants warm their toes in winter at a square section adobe fireplace, jutting out from a corner on a slightly raised hearth. In the more prosperous country villas of Italy and Spain you are likely to find a broad fireplace, possibly decorated with tiles, supporting a wide mantlepiece. Carved stone and marble are used generously in these regions where the materials are readily available and an artisan tradition persists. Many Italian homes have a blue and white tiled *stufa*, or stove, with matching fireplace surrounds, as well as grandiose carved stone mantles supported by curvy herms. In Tuscany, fireplaces of plainly carved stone are often broad and high, the interiors painted white as a frame for a surprisingly small raised fire area. They become an architectural feature with gravitas, even when the fire is unlit. If they have the money, Italians may prefer pink marble, with ornate salmon and white stucco depicting crests and coats of arms as the essential mantle decor.

Flanked by French windows, corner fireplaces of the utmost simplicity have a prestige in Spanish country houses, though there are flamboyant examples favouring the grotesque and the Baroque. In southern Spain, glazed majolica tiles and adobe make a link with Mexico, and even today rural houses are never without the *mesa camilla* – a round table with a heavy tablecloth – under which is set a metal bowl of hot coals.

Left Colourful patterned tiles cover the entire interior of this fireplace. Such grand designs were often commissioned for the opulent homes of wealthy Italians.

Top right *Stufas* are often incredibly impressive pieces of furniture; their very size and beautiful majolica tiles make them an object of admiration as well as warmth.

Bottom right This rustic adobe fireplace is typical of the fireplaces found in the hotter parts of southern Europe. The white plaster walls are cool in summer, but the large square opening emits ample heat on those chillier winter evenings.

IN FRANCE, THE country houses of Brittany and Normandy have mortared raw stone fireplaces, with or without a massive oak lintel. These huge fireplaces are very wide and raised, sometimes to waist height in dining rooms for cooking purposes. Grander homes have a simple but dignified sculpted fireplace with a mantle reaching to the ceiling. These fireplaces may be made from carved grey stone, heavily patterned marble, or even plaster painted in lapis lazuli. The French use an attractive detail of fine herringbone tile laid on edge for the back and base of the fire, or majolica tiles for the surround, matched by the tiles on the hearth. Forever practical, they tend to combine several uses, and manor house kitchens have vast fireplaces of stone incorporating beehive-shaped *potagers* (niches where a casserole simmers throughout the day).

northern Europe

The French have a passion for stoves, and France is the birthplace of the ornate, cylindrical Godin stove. This may be set into an existing fireplace, its functionality softened by a feminine touch of lace across the mantlepiece. Stoves can be tall phallic structures in bright green enamel or black Gothic, hefty masculine and utilitarian Danish woodburners, or thoroughly workmanlike culinary altars – huge, shining black machines, handsomely trimmed in shining brass. The further north you go in Europe, to Holland, Switzerland, Scandinavia, Austria and Germany, the more likely it is that heating will come from stoves. Cleaner and more economical, they do not involve an open chimney down which draughts are apt to scud, and are evidently safer in houses constructed from wood.

There is a Scandinavian tradition for tall, cylindrical corner stoves, entirely clad in curved tiles manufactured by Store Kongensgade in Copenhagen and specially designed for the purpose; these stoves consist of a plinth from which the stove rises, with two metal doors for the fire. But fireplaces are also part of the Swedish vernacular, particularly in sociable rooms that are cheered by an open fire blazing in a fine Gustavian surround of blue and white tiles and a shallow ceramic mantle. A tradition of cooking indoors on open flames has resulted in ingenious and sculptural plaster barbecues, cleverly incorporating shelves and niches for wine bottles, casseroles and logs. Tiled stoves reached their peak in Austria with the stunningly elaborate relief polychrome example that radiates warmth in the Golden Room of Hohensalsburg, standing proudly on a menagerie of smiling lions.

Top left Stoves are ever popular across northern Europe, where unpredictable weather patterns demand a source of heat that is less hard work than an open fire.

Top right In France, a simple oak lintel tops a functional block fireplace, with an ingenious chain holding in the logs stacked neatly to the side.

Bottom left Carefully preserved in the Golden Room of Hohensalsburg in Austria, this tiled stove is a sight to behold.

Bottom right Beautifully maintained, this cast-iron stove takes pride of place among traditional blue and white tiles in a Dutch café.

the Americas

IN MEXICO, THE remnants of Spanish culture have transmuted over time. As a result, the Mexican adobe fireplace is more sculptural, rounded and less rectilinear than its European ancestor. Typically it stands in a corner, with the hearth raised above floor level on a plinth, which may be painted. There is a simple, arched opening for the fire, and a solid stepped mantleshelf above. The appearance is comforting and satisfying, and painted religious icons or bleached buffalo skulls tend to be optional extras.

The rounded adobe barbecue, familiar from many an American do-it-yourself manual, started life in Mexico. Its purpose was not necessarily just culinary, as there is every reason to spend the scintillating indigo nights sitting outside, talking, drinking, singing, particularly if you have an outdoor fireplace for warmth and focus. It is a fashion that has caught fire in North America too, taken to extremes, where in many houses massive brick hearths adjoin external walls, and adobe fireplaces are used to warm the houses.

In Mexico, where brilliant *azulejos* (a continuum from their Spanish and Portuguese antecedents) are a rainbow component of interiors and a jazzy alternative to smooth white painted adobe, tiled fireplaces and stoves are a familiar kitchen feature. Generally, plain coloured, glazed squares are used in a two-coloured checked pattern, covering every available surface, including the arched alcove and adjoining worktops. Occasionally, in more affluent households, patterned tiles are used, or a bold and celebratory patchwork of almost every colour under the sun. Finishing is an important and carefully considered matter, and there is a distant hint of Islam in the borders, edgings, covings and geometry of tiny tiles set to complete the design and mark transitions from one surface to another.

Top left Natural materials can be incredibly colourful, as is evident in this Frank Lloyd Wright fireplace where stone abounds.

Bottom left The influence of Spain and Portugal in South America led to the proliferation of adobe fireplaces.

A Fireplace for your Home

Finding and fitting a fireplace can be a pleasure. It is an exercise that spans the practical and the fantastical, you can indulge in dreams as well as consider the stark practicalities of back boilers and solid fuel. If your taste is for the formal and your furniture has heirloom status, you may want to delve in antique shops and architectural salvage warehouses. If a romantic heart beats within, you might consider something more rustic, sculpted out of adobe, or more outrageous, clad entirely in twinkling mosaic.

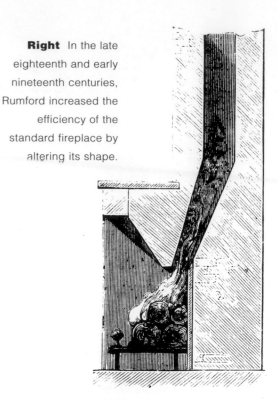

Right In the late eighteenth and early nineteenth centuries, Rumford increased the efficiency of the standard fireplace by altering its shape.

the perfect fireplace

THE FIRST ESSENTIAL for an effective fireplace is a good draught, and this, in part, is a product of a good chimney. A good chimney is well insulated and runs up within the house, so that the flue gases remain warm until they reach the very top. This should be the highest point of the building, to prevent problems with downwinds. If possible, the flue pipe should run directly upwards, without offsets or changes in direction, either of which impede the upward progress of gases.

The second prerequisite concerns the balance of air coming and going within the house. This boils down to ensuring that the fireplace or stove and chimney are well sealed, and that the house has a balanced ventilation system – undeflected by a heavy-duty kitchen exhaust fan, for example, which will depressurise the air within the house, making an open fire impossible to run efficiently.

Finally, you should ascertain that the stove or fireplace is certified for low smoke emissions. Alternatively, if you are starting from scratch, you could investigate the acclaimed Rumford fireplace. This piece of history – first put into practice in 1796 – has been resuscitated, and the components are being manufactured today. The hearth is tall and conveniently shallow, taking a much smaller bite out of the room than a conventional fireplace. It has widely splayed covings to reflect heat efficiently to the room, and cunning engineering within the chimney to ensure maximum heat, while obviating smoke, draughts and wastage.

Below A well-built chimney is essential for a good draw on a fire.

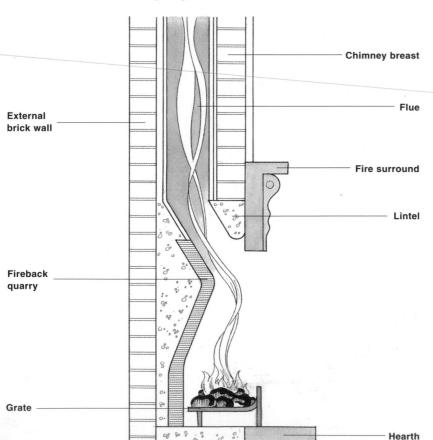

Chimney breast

Flue

Fire surround

Lintel

External brick wall

Fireback quarry

Grate

Hearth

installing a fireplace

BUILDING A FIREPLACE from scratch is a highly specialised job, and, for safety reasons, not one that an amateur should undertake. But fitting a prefabricated grate into an existing fireplace is manageable, as is fixing or changing a mantlepiece. Whatever style of mantlepiece you choose, make sure that it is in proportion to the chimney breast. Ideally try to find one that has the same measurements as the previous one, but better too large than too small. Check, particularly if you are buying secondhand, that all the parts are there, and that you can make sense of the base, which is where mantles often suffer during a move. If you have managed to find an antique marble mantle, this will probably come as a bundle of unidentified strips, and you will have to use every iota of brainpower to fathom exactly what goes where, and which way up. Pay attention to the hearthstone, and investigate stone, slate and tile if you need to replace the original. Find a fender that fits exactly to give a neat finish. And, if you opt for gas or coal, look out for well-designed matching paraphernalia, though all those tongs, shovels, scuttles and pokers will be unnecessary if you decide to have a fake fire.

Gas-fired coal is highly efficient, and looks so similar to the real thing that your problem will be to stop guests throwing junk mail and cigarette butts into the flames, which might block the gas outlet. Such a fire can be fitted with minimum disruption to an existing fireplace, with just a slender copper pipe to betray its fuel source. However, you will have to live with a pile of less than attractive, and often dusty, 'coals' in summer when the fire is out of use. This is a small price to pay for inexpensive, adjustable heat, and total

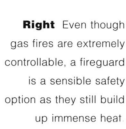

Right Even though gas fires are extremely controllable, a fireguard is a sensible safety option as they still build up immense heat.

Right A large number of components make up the complicated anatomy of a fireplace, which has hardly changed since the fifteenth century.

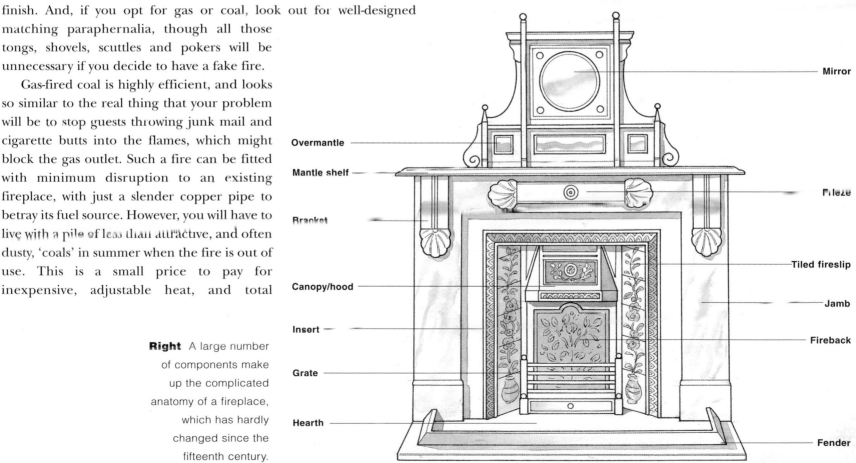

Mirror

Overmantle

Mantle shelf

Frieze

Bracket

Tiled fireslip

Canopy/hood

Jamb

Insert

Fireback

Grate

Hearth

Fender

Above Fake coals are so similar to real coals that it is often difficult to tell whether a fire is gas or solid fuel.

convenience. In a city, one would need convincing reasons to ignore the advantages of fake fuel. In the country, where wood is sometimes available at no expense, smells divine, and makes a livelier conflagration, you would need good reasons to look elsewhere. If you want real fuel, the questions you must ask are, do you want to experiment with a shallow and carefully engineered Rumford fireplace or stick with convention? If the former, then you will have to find a supplier of the constituents or a builder who understands the principles. Chimneys must conform with safety regulations, and if yours is an existing chimney, it will need to be checked and cleared. Do you want wood or coal? How easy is fuel to buy, can it be delivered, how much does it cost, and where will you store it?

Woodburning stoves need different treatment as they work on the principle of controlled combustion. This means that you can regulate the airflow and control the speed at which the fuel burns, and therefore how much heat the stove gives out. Heat-circulating stoves draw cold air in at the bottom between the firebox and the casing, heat it, and then expel it as warm air at the top. When buying a stove, consider the number of windows you have, the insulation, and the floor area. Also take into account that old stoves will not be as airtight as new ones. Maintenance is easy – you will need to clear the ashes from time to time, and a capacious ash drawer is handy for this, as well as a large door, since it is a bore to have to chop logs into very small pieces. There are ingenious heat exchangers to extract the maximum heat from the installation, and water heaters, both of which are attached to the flue pipe. You can even find flue ovens, if you are really determined, so it pays to do some initial research before buying.

Top left This sleek ultramodern stove ensures that the dust and ash that wood fires notoriously create are not a problem.

Top right A roaring log fire is an unbeatable presence, whatever the style of your home.

the warmth of wood

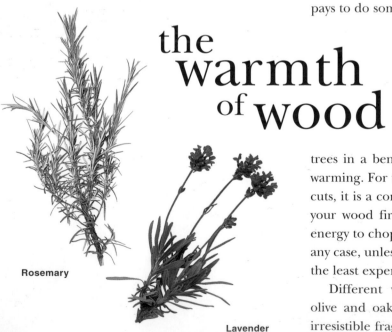

Rosemary

Lavender

AS WELL AS its intrinsic merits, a fire of burning logs has ecological advantages over fossil fuel. Wood is a renewable resource and, although the heat it generates does emit carbon dioxide, this is absorbed by growing trees in a benign cycle that does not ultimately contribute to global warming. For those who live in the wilds, subject to weather and power cuts, it is a comfort to know that when everything else has shut down, your wood fire will just burn all the brighter. And, if you have the energy to chop and transport it, you can find wood to burn for free. In any case, unless you live in the middle of a city, a load of wood is one of the least expensive forms of heating.

Different woods have various burning qualities. For example, olive and oak burn slowly, whereas pine burns fast and exudes an irresistible fragrance. Fruit wood taken from prunings and dead trees

Bottom left The fireside tools of brush and shovel are essential for an open coal fire.

Bottom right Small logs are necessary to fit into the mouth of this unusual and colorful ceramic 'fire pot'.

a fireplace for your home

Left The powerful
light that the flames
of burning logs emit
has an innate cosiness
that is impossible
to replicate with
electric light.

has a sweet smell and, providing it is dry, burns beautifully. Superstition forbids the burning of elm, in which the spirits of witches are traditionally supposed to reside until unleashed by fire. Many superstitions have a basis in fact, and elm is generally too sappy to burn well.

There is something about an open fire that demands attention and feeding. It takes real self-control simply to sit by a fire and not fidget with it. So, if you feel the need to tamper with it, you might bring in a supply of aromatic woody herbs to scent the room – sprigs of rosemary, lavender and bay thrown on the flames will make the room smell like an aromatherapy session.

building a fire

THE CLASSIC METHOD of building a fire is with a neat pile of crumpled paper beneath a wigwam of kindling, upon which larger logs are balanced precariously. One lit match, and with a favourable draught, the fire should spring into life. In practice, it often seems to be more complicated than this and, in desperation, you may find yourself expending the contents of an entire box of firelighters on getting the fire started. There is a new school of thought that radically challenges ancient habits. This involves building the fire from the base upwards, using large logs as a foundation and diminishing their size as you build, finishing off with tinder and paper. This effective technique can be used on open fires and in stoves. Surprisingly, it works a treat, though it is essential to have fine, dry and flammable kindling at the top. In addition, it minimises smoke and the structure does not collapse on itself and smother the flames.

Above If you believe in witches, then remember not to burn elm as you may just conjure up some unwanted visitors.

Right There are two opposing ways of building a fire; the more traditional one being that illustrated on the far right.

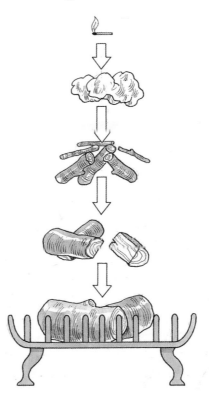

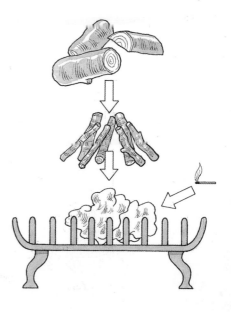

old or new?

ANTIQUE OR SECONDHAND fireplaces can be found at auction, though they may need repair and will probably not come cheap. You can buy the whole kit, from an ornate, carved Victorian rosewood fire surround and overmantle, complete with carved birds and bone inlay, to a seventeenth-century cast-iron fireback depicting Susanna and the Elders. The former may set you back the cost of a small new car, the latter a long-haul plane flight. If you do have the money, you will get character, quality, style and grace by buying antique. Unless you have a brand new house, an old fireplace will look more authentic, simply because it will have signs of wear and use, though modern replicas can be almost indistinguishable from the real thing.

It is a good idea to check out houses of the same vintage in the neighbourhood, to see if they have original fireplaces. Measure them if you can, and if you manage to find something the same size it will look far more convincing than getting the era correct but the size wrong. With a nineteenth-century fireplace in particular, you may have a problem matching the height of the skirting board with its base. It takes persistence to find matching register grates. If you go for a freestanding grate, again you have to keep an eye on proportion.

On the other hand, new fireplaces can be obtained that imitate any look or era you fancy, at a fraction of the cost of the genuine article. Or, at the fashionable end of modern design, they can be as exciting as sculptures in concrete or steel. They do not have to be at floor level, and there are ingenious designs that disappear discreetly when not in use, or that you can use to cook upon. The vital thing to bear in mind is proportion. Never position a tiny fireplace in a large room, or vice versa.

You need to consult your bank balance, assess your overall style, and weigh up the era and finish of the house. Finally, picture your dream of the perfect fireplace and how you wish to enjoy it.

Top left The most unusual fireplaces can be found lying among piles of rotting and rusting furniture in architectural salvage yards.

Bottom left Fireplaces have been entirely rethought by today's designers, and can compete with any other futuristic elements you may have in your home.

Top left Fireplaces became such a focus for the home in the nineteenth century that homeowners were bombarded with choice.

Far left Stylish reproductions can be purchased in all styles, and the Tudor look is particularly popular.

Bottom left Architectural salvage yards are treasure troves for fireplaces of all periods and materials, and great fun can be had finding your dream fireplace.

a fireplace for your home

make it
personal

THE HUNT FOR the appropriate fireplace or stove is, or should be, a pleasurable task, and the most important factor by far is that you feel happy with your choice. Always consult your heart – your feelings, as well as judgment, are paramount. The decisions are fairly basic, and can be blithely ignored if you have a contrary passion to work against the architectural style of your home. As a rough guideline, one can generalise about urban or countrified, authentic period or modern, colourful or discreet, roughly handmade or sharply industrial, functional or whimsical. A stove may suit your needs best, depending on the availability of fuel and how much warmth you want for your labours. In certain less used and private rooms, such as bedrooms or bathrooms, gas-fired fakes are ideal. In such circumstances, they are the best and most luxurious invention.

Some materials, such as marble, have an innate and citified sophistication, and will look out of place in a humble rustic setting. Similarly, adobe or rough-hewn wooden lintels will do your city dwelling no favours. Ornate Victorian interiors with dadoes, moulding, picture rails and cornices, can take a fireplace with curlicues as well as an opulent mirror above. Alternatively, you can create a pool of relative peace in the hectic decor by choosing something plain and as large as the room can take. Victorian architecture has a breezy confidence, which means it seems to be able to absorb anything and retain its own character.

As for pre-Victorian times, an attempt at striking the right era is advisable. The most demanding period is neatly symmetrical Georgian – in deference to what is widely considered the golden age of domestic architecture, you should rigorously research any possible fireplace you wish to install.

The twentieth century is almost as problematic. Where the architecture is pared down and simplified, any additions demand attention. If you are determined to have an Adam fireplace in your 1950s flat, make it a sizeable one and follow it through with a handsome register grate. On the other hand, you can paint a plain wooden fireplace with shapely caryatids, or trompe l'oeil columns if you prefer. Confine the colours of fireplace and accessories to a few shades to give coherence.

The surround is part of the problem, and the fireplace within is the remainder. Grates and firebacks are less noticeable, being for the most part black iron and recessed. However, if you manage to find a stylistic common denominator – delicacy or machismo, generosity or neatness – you will be halfway there. Just take courage, and prepare to enjoy the finished hybrid.

Left Paint your fireplace to meld in with the overall colour scheme of your room, and you will have automatically created a very soothing space.

Top right A big fire for a big room; if you have the space, be bold and install something worthy of the room.

Bottom right Personalise your fireplace with ornaments and photos that retain happy memories for you.

Right This
ostentatious fireplace is
a fine example of
fireplace design taken
to the extreme.

The Evolution of the Fireplace

With all that the twenty-first century has to offer in terms of luxury and pastimes, few of us can claim that we are not lured into a sense of relaxation by a fire, or that we do not relish the smell of a barbecue on a summer's evening. Fire, albeit controlled, is still a desirable element, even though it may be only an occasional fancy rather than a daily necessity. Hence, the evolution of fireplaces intrigues as we are still very much in touch with our ancestors' needs and desires in this sphere.

chapter 1

Early Fireplaces

In order to serve the dual function of cooking and warming the household, the first formalised fireplaces – that is, against a solid wall – often had very large openings. Such openings enabled large groups to gather around and numerous items to be cooked over the flames simultaneously.

Fire is a tricky element to control – too little attention and it dies, too much fuel and oxygen and it can rampage. The earliest fireplaces were mere piles of timber sited in the middle of a large space, well away from the inflammable walls of yurt, cabin or hut. Among nomadic people this system is still maintained. Chimneys of drystone or rocks evolved to channel the smoke and facilitate cooking, until gradually it became a structural component of the building and recognisable as what is thought of as a fireplace today. Decorative surrounds are believed to have first appeared around the twelfth century. However, it is well known that ancient cave drawings were probably lit up by fires, and could, therefore, be seen as fireplace art,

central
fires

FROM THE EARLIEST settlements, the houses of the poor were built simply using any materials available – stone, wattle and daub, cob and turf, with a structural framework of logs or wooden poles – and most lacked niceties in the way of chimneys and hearths. Typical early structures were often a small, rustic A-framed room, with few windows and no chimney. As the wooden framework was combustible, the fire – a smoky, choking pile of logs smouldering in the middle of a floor of beaten earth – was built well away from the walls. There may have been basic ventilation in the roof to allow the smoke to escape, with the fire raised on stones or contained within a pit. In stony parts of the country, the house of poles and turf would have had a stone chimney attached to one side. In a larger house, the smoke from the central fire would eddy out through chinks in roof tiles, louvres or gablets, leaving blackened traces of its passage on the roof beams. As houses became more sophisticated with the addition of extra storeys, smoke had to find its way out through a smoke bay, which evolved into chimney and flues. Those who plundered, fought or traded their way to wealth would have had similar structures in grander, less smoky, and probably chillier rooms. The medieval great hall had height and space, a proper floor of brick or stone and a large central hearth upon which huge logs burned on massive andirons. The smoke escaped through a louvred hole in the centre of the ceiling, and at the end of the day, there was sure to have been a chilly sprint to the comforts of the heavily curtained four-poster.

Top left The dome-shaped teepee, usually constructed from wood and animal skin, was characteristic of the homes of the Cree tribe of North America. Within these often surprisingly large structures, a central fire, ventilated by a hole at the top of the structure, would warm and feed entire families.

Bottom left The climate of Kamchatka, a province in the far east of the former USSR, required the locals to retain fireplaces in their spartan, thatched summer dwellings. Although this fire appears to be located dangerously near the side of the hut, a wide, open doorway and a hole in the roof add light and ventilation.

Right Central fires or stoves are the perfect answer for modern open-plan homes, bringing warmth and comfort to large, airy spaces.

from the Normans to the Tudors

GRAND NORMAN FIREPLACES, like Norman churches, had rounded stone arches, often with a semicircular space in which to build a fire. Massive stone or plaster and timber hoods were first built at around this time, with the great advantage that the eye-watering smoke from damp timber could be induced to go up into the night air rather than into the faces of the assembled gathering. Most fireplaces were plain with a delicate lintel, and lined with clay, brick or plaster. As the single most imposing feature in a lordly chamber, they began to parade the ornate handiwork of conspicuous wealth, with elaborate carvings, coats of arms, corbels and other fancy details. Some owners had several fireplaces in a single room, or the fireplace might simply be big enough to accommodate an entire tree to warm an unruly retinue. Carving in stone and oak was a luxury that only the wealthiest could afford, but where they could, they flaunted it, and magnificent fireplaces still remain in surprising numbers.

Gradually, fortified castles at the noble end of the scale, and shanty dwellings at the peasant end, were replaced with manor houses and cottages, all of which would have had several fireplaces. By the sixteenth century, fireplaces were higher and wider in order to heat lofty spaces and burn hefty logs. They were also neatly placed against a wall with all the functional additions of chimneys – mantles, hearths and hoods.

Left The huge plaster hood of this Italian fireplace proudly displays the ancient coat of arms of a powerful family. The large opening has been blocked in – probably to stop the rain and wind from pouring down the huge chimney. The increasing use of hoods and canopies – which cleverly channelled smoke out of the room – in the fifteenth century, led to the relocation of the fireplace from the middle of the room to the wall.

Bottom right The simple decoration on this Tudor arch was more typical of early Tudor fireplaces before pomp and ceremony took precedent.

a hole in the wall

THE MODERATELY WEALTHY, who had no coat of arms to parade above the flames, made of the fireplace a tiny, low-ceilinged room – the so-called, beloved inglenook – where they could sit and roast their toes while wiping their watering eyes. Convivial drinkers could plunge the fire-warmed, red-hot poker into their flagons and make, with a sprinkling of spices, mulled cider or beer to warm their bellies. A simple wooden lintel, sometimes chamfered, moulded or carved, and now rock-hard with age and tempered by heat and smoke, supported the wall above. Within the firebrick-lined and -floored fireplace there may be cupboards and niches for storing logs, tinder, kindling and salt.

These fireplaces served a dual purpose – cooking and heating. Hooks nailed into the lintel held bulky kitchen pans, and a swivelling crane swung out from the alcove to hold and manoeuvre heavier iron pots, raised and lowered by means of a metal ratchet. The open hearth has not changed greatly, but what has altered, with the vagaries of fashion and the availability of fuel, is the appearance. For almost all sections of society, the fireplace developed from a basic hole in the wall to a showy altar, resplendent with carved stone or a cheaper, dense form of chalk, the gleam of polished oak or marble, heraldic devices and precious objects.

Right Early large brick-lined fireplaces with a brick hearth were built purely for function rather than aesthetics.

COOKING IMPLEMENTS

The old-fashioned array of iron pots and kettles was suspended over the flames on chains and adjustable trammels, or sat on an iron rack over the fire. Narrow ovens were often built into the walls on each side of the fireplace, and special flat shovels, called *peles*, were used to retrieve loaves set to bake at the back of the oven. Meat was roasted on spits, and, over time, devices were designed to keep the spit turning to ensure even cooking.

Top left A peat-burning cottage fireplace combines old-fashioned cooking implements with the early twentieth-century fashion of a tiled surround.

Bottom left The basic principle of a hole-in-the-wall worked so well that examples can be found all over the world; this one is in Spain.

A big pot, ideal for making a large hotpot to feed the whole family.

This kettle is typical of those found on nineteenth-century cooking ranges.

The long handle of these brass pans allowed them to be placed deep into the fire, but still be retrieved safely.

the Tudors & the Elizabethans

THE ELIZABETHANS HAD great belief in self-promotion – names, crests, mottoes, family trees, adventures and marriages were emblazoned on chimneypieces, firebacks, lintels, jambs and anywhere else a craftsman could fit them. The Tudor explosion of wealth, combined with massive egos and elaborate self-glorification, resulted in a great legacy of ornamented overmantles, all rich with anecdote. Their vigour, character and attention to both the grand effect and the smallest detail is truly inspiring. Even those with the most creative bent will find them hard to replicate at home, but the three-dimensional stone and wood motifs and designs, edgings and patterns can be copied for use in two dimensions in the humbler medium of paint. Recurrent motifs that were randomly combined above and beside the typical four-centred fireplace arch – virgins, caryatids, crests, initials, scrolls, crests, medallions, panels, crenellated and dentil edgings, strapwork, flowers, mythical beasts and obelisks – were borrowed from the overflowing Tudor pattern book or from the Renaissance craftsmen who carved so many fireplaces.

Top left A handsome pastiche of a traditional four-centred arch fireplace, slightly diminished in size to fit into a contemporary home.

Top right Crisply carved and simply constructed – a confident twenty-first-century version of an historic mantelpiece. Such excellent reproductions illustrate that stone-carving is, fortunately, not a lost art.

Top left Intricate carving was a common feature on Tudor fireplaces, and can be finely reproduced today.

Top right Long, low and wide – such fireplaces required the space of a great hall and the wood of a forest.

Bottom left Ornately carved Tudor symbols on a heavy overmantle clearly date this fireplace.

Bottom right The fireplaces of less wealthy persons were simply carved, with little ornamentation, perhaps just a discreet pair of medallions.

Bottom left The turn of the seventeenth century saw a plethora of intricately carved, highly decorative overmantles, which almost always bore the coat of arms of the household. This fine example is joined by a pair of equally resplendent silver andirons.

Bottom right A Tudorbethan reproduction fireplace, complete with carved corners, takes on the modern safety features of a raised plinth and built-in fire screen.

Puritan
style

PURITAN STYLE TRAVELLED across the Atlantic to New England, its hallmarks being austerity, simplicity and modesty. Wood – oak, chestnut and walnut for the structure, and cedar for floors and roof shingles – was the likeliest building material. The chimney was a major structural element in the early timber-framed houses, with chimney girts – heavy beams that ran across the length of the house – abutting the chimney on either side. In the seventeenth century, the fireplaces tended to be massive, back-to-back and central, and this combination of features must have contributed to the eight great fires that swept across Boston in its first sixty years. The fireplace dominating the multipurpose room or hall could be as wide as eight feet, and was used not only to warm the occupants, but also to cook food on the built-in brick oven.

On arrival on this alien shore, there were more pressing priorities for the Pilgrim Fathers than constructing a grand mantlepiece, and niceties were pushed aside by the labour of survival. The Pilgrims had little spare energy, time or materials, and were not of a luxury loving disposition; so the simple yet elegant panelled wooden fireplace surround that matched the interior finish of the room made the best use of the abundant raw materials to hand, and was a natural and graceful solution that has endured.

Left The solid wood lintel above this early fireplace melds into its surroundings, as the rest of the house appears to be made mostly from timber. Bread would have been baked in the square alcove at the back of the hearth.

Left The once-essential kitchen utensils surrounding this simple fireplace are its only form of decoration.

chapter 2

France, Italy & the Grand Style

The grand palaces of Europe took interior decoration to new heights during the Renaissance. The Palazzo della Farnesina in Rome was no exception – this salon has no surface free of adornment. Trompe l'oeil pillars rise out of the multicoloured marble floor and walls, and an imposing painting decorates the chimney hood.

In Europe, splendour and opulence in the seventeenth and eighteenth centuries were usually advertised by copious use of carved marble in the classical and flamboyant ornamentation of Baroque and rococo. Doorframes, floors, pillars, altars and fireplaces all gleamed with the chilly pallor of Tuscan Carrara marble, or the richness of the basic calcite with a whole palette of enhancing impurities, such as green with terra verde and red with iron oxide. Different marbles were combined in overweening compositions, with breathtaking craftsmanship and a satisfying excess of gilding, carving and adornment. Such excess was for the greater glory of French and Italian aristocrats, whose palaces were stunningly and perfectly executed with schemes of idolatrous richness.

grandiloquent
Baroque

Top left This bold fireplace has all the Baroque motifs – swirling columns, hefty dentils, faux tree trunks above and barleysugar pillars below.

Bottom left Cylindrical obelisks topped by acorns, gilded ram's horns and lounging putti – this Italian fireplace from the Palazzo Ducale Urbino displays the Baroque love of detail.

THE BAROQUE MOVEMENT was spawned as a clarion call by the Catholics of Rome in the mid-seventeenth century. It is architecture as strip cartoon, as poster and propaganda, and to more puritan sensibilities its richness is excessive. Classically-inspired, but utterly flamboyant, 'over the top' probably best describes it, and there is always a suspicion of the meretricious with Baroque. Lovers of kitsch will adore it.

The word 'baroque' originally meant 'misshapen', as applied to the giant pearls that seventeenth-century jewellers liked to fashion into the torso of a Triton or the headdress of a hippocamp. Regular geometry was abandoned by architects who made adventurous forays into curves and undulations, gilded barleysugar pilasters, and painted fake perspectives.

Fireplaces did not escape this theatrical passion for contortion and trumpery, and at their most triumphantly Baroque they were enormous and curvaceous, with abundant folderols of bronze, gilt and marble, flanked by voluptuous caryatids and topped by a trompe l'oeil painting of buxom draped women.

Right A strong sense of design holds a multiplicity of elements in control here, with painted panels articulating the walls and outlining the chimney breast above a curvaceous marble fireplace.

romantic rococo

EVENTUALLY THERE WAS a penchant for something a little less serious than neoclassicism, and rococo was born. Europe – France, Austria and Germany in particular – fell prey to a passion for rococo in the 1730s, and since America and Great Britain had really missed out on Baroque with its Catholic connotations, rococo was adopted with alacrity as a witty and elegant substitute.

After centuries of hard, dark, rectangular and masculine architecture, rococo was a more feminine movement that showed itself in touches of lightness, delicacy and decorative charm. The term comes from the French 'rocaille', meaning 'rock-work' or 'shell-work', which gave rise to a style of interior decoration based on S-shaped sweeps and low-relief scroll-like forms. Bright colours, light woods and the exotic were the order of the day, while the elements, the seasons and Aesop's fables were popular themes. Walls and ceilings were embellished with continuous foliage, shells or abstract shapes, and symmetry gave way to sinuous, organic curves.

Top left The mottled, coffee-coloured marble of this fireplace is well-matched by the tan leather of the late-addition fender.

Top right The curvaceous rococo fire basket is in perfect keeping with the impressive, shapely mantlepiece that surrounds it.

Bottom left A cast-iron Victorian reproduction of a rococo fireplace is festooned with the tendrils and curlicues of rococo style.

Bottom right A fine plaster reproduction rococo fireplace, all feminine curls and flowers, holding its own in a strong masculine decor.

FIRE BASKETS

Fire baskets were designed for hearths that burned coal. Typically made of wrought iron, their purpose was to prevent the hot coals from falling forward onto the floor. On occasion, these baskets incorporated useful receptacles for fireside tools such as bellows, tongs, shovels and brushes, while on others places for warming bottles and jugs of wine were incorporated into the design.

Coals could be piled high safely, while gaps in the basket's front allowed access for pokers.

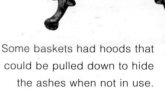

Some baskets had hoods that could be pulled down to hide the ashes when not in use.

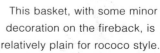

This basket, with some minor decoration on the fireback, is relatively plain for rococo style.

3

Georgian &
Regency Styles

This beautiful, understated Regency fireplace is enhanced by its surroundings – the furniture dates from a similar period and an ambience of comfortable luxury is present in this Regency-style room.

The Georgian period extended from 1714 to the accession of Queen Victoria to the English throne in 1837. It came as a reaction to the fevered excesses of Baroque, and was everything that Baroque was not. With a passion for restrained and exquisitely proportioned work, the Georgians adopted with enthusiasm the grand, measured and symmetrical style of ancient Rome and Greece. From 1725 onwards, columns and capitals, caryatids and acanthus leaves began to spring up in the most unlikely places, including fireplaces. The Regency period from 1811 to 1820 (when George, the Prince of Wales, acted as regent for his father, George III) was, following the dignity, proportion and decorum of the Georgians, a time of expensive frivolity, marked by a passion for the exotic.

architectural
&sculptural
influences

Top left Classical restraint was often a defining feature of Georgian fireplaces, and the fireplace became a physically less obtrusive part of the room. A narrow shelf would be supported by architectural jambs, all made of white marble.

Bottom left Regency style took the classical form to its height with simple, rectilinear forms, reeded jambs and corner roundels.

THE GREAT GEORGIAN houses were conceived as an architectural whole, resulting in a homogeneity quite unlike the patchwork of plundered bits and pieces that were cobbled together in previous buildings. Eighteenth-century architects were the film stars of their day, celebrated and plagiarised in equal measure. The works of William Kent and Robert Adam (who had researched in Italy) in Britain, and James Gibbs in America, became widely known and fashionable via their published works. William Chambers's *Treatise on Civil Architecture* was one of many hugely influential reference works whose illustrations became blueprints for architectural detail on both sides of the Atlantic. Under these architects' direction, continued chimneypieces, in which the chimney breast flowed from floor to ceiling is a single composition, became the vogue, as contrasted with simple chimneypieces, in which the decoration ended at the mantleshelf.

Mirrors, paintings, stucco panels and bas-relief carvings were incorporated in the overmantle design. Sculptors were commissioned to carve grandiose chimneypieces depicting scenes of Roman heroes in togas, or painters decorated the ornately framed space above the fireplace with flowers, fruit or landscapes. Such grandeur filtered down to the moderately wealthy, who instructed their builders to add pilasters, stone insets or mouldings to their own specifications in main rooms. But fires in secondary rooms and bedrooms were smaller, narrower and unadorned, and the plain terraced houses of the majority had fireplaces set unobtrusively into panelled wood, with only a wooden lip above the fire, if anything at all.

Right The delicate bas-relief on the frieze is an understated example of the designs that Robert Adam was renowned for.

use of marble

IF MONEY WAS no object, white, grey or black marble was the favoured choice. Marble is heavy, durable, and can be carved and polished. Its different colours, streaks and featherings are due to mineral impurities. It was a great discovery by eighteenth-century architects, and craftsmen fashioned it in every kind of decorative two- and three-dimensional manner. William Kent used black and gold Carrara marbles, paler around the fireplace, with a dark pediment above.

For reasons of economy, and because some marbles are strongly patterned, there might just be a slender framework of the precious material set into something plainer and cheaper. When marble was used together with wood, carved or otherwise, the wood was almost always painted. Alternatively, the craftsmen of the day might have embellished the wood with relief motifs of gesso, or a soft metal such as pewter, which was applied and then painted.

Italian marble was prized, but so too were the quiet, subtle colours of English igneous minerals, such as feldspar, Derbyshire alabaster – also known as Blue John – and Purbeck stone. But not all could afford these luxurious materials, and the middle classes often chose to use scagliola (gypsum and aggregates mixed with glue), polished to a heady sheen to resemble the cool grandeur of marble.

Left Colour bursts out of this fantastic marble fireplace, which has a wealth of texture and depth created by the incredibly rich patterned marble.

Top right The heavy vein in this plain marble adds an acceptable element of decoration to this sleek look.

Bottom right The simple style of early Georgian classical fireplaces – narrow shelf, plain scrolls – is easily reproduced, as is this dark marble with its wonderfully rich heavy veining. The simplicity is beautifully adorned by finely crafted furniture and pale amethyst walls.

Adam's use of colour

Top right This fireplace, designed by Robert Adam himself, is very much part of a whole room set. The pastels of the decorative inlays on the fireplace are repeated on the nearby doorframe, while the rich colours of the surrounding walls are heightened by the delicacy of the fireplace colours and decoration.

ROBERT ADAM SUBJECTED marble to a variety of different treatments. His are the intricate marble inlays of contrasting colours, or the combinations of different hues to add architectural emphasis. Fillets of dark marble might frame the fire, with a paler marble surround, possibly with fluted columns inlaid with colored 'compo'. White statuary marble was often used by Adam, enriched with 'antique incrustations', such as classical crowd scenes in low relief, or consoles bearing the carved heads of rams. He left no detail unconsidered, and the grates he designed were apt to gleam with burnished steel and brass, echoing the use of ormolu (gilded brass or bronze used for decoration) on the mantles.

Fireplaces were designed to marry with doors and other architectural details, and where possible the same materials were used for both. Scrolls or pediments would also echo each other, drawing the room into a unified whole. In addition, under Robert Adam's influence, mantlepieces were made deeper to accommodate mirrors and ornaments, which further continued the harmonisation of colours and materials. Adam was an extraordinary colourist, and whereas his fireplaces tended to keep the natural colours of the materials, they were set in contexts of rich burgundy silk hangings, or in rooms where the 'grounds of the panels and friezes are coloured with light tints of pink and green, so as to take the glare off the white'. Rose pink, lilac, bright blue, yellow, greens, dusty orange and turquoise were some of the fresh and unexpected colours he used, even going so far as to tint the Chippendale woodwork blue to tone with the fabrics he wished to use.

Below The rich, colourful marble inlaid into the corner of the mantle forms a stunning background for high relief, intricately carved marble details – this magnificent detail has Robert Adam's signature all over it.

Far right The Greek-inspired bold profiles and high relief are shown to their best advantage through the use of pure white marble.

Bottom right Architect Sir John Soane was strongly influenced by Robert Adam. In this fireplace in Soane's London house, we can see how Soane took on board Adam's use of colour – the entire room has been painted to match the fireplace surround.

John Soane & the end of the Regency

THE REGENCY WAS a wonderful era for the wealthy amateur, who could dabble in an astonishing repertoire of architectural styles. He might dream up a sanitised version of Gothic, or he might have caught sight of Piranesi's book on Egyptian motifs and decided to adorn his fireplace with hawks, sphinxes, crocodile details and obelisks. Perhaps a rich individual's eclectic search for the sublime might have led him to China or the Indies, and resulted in a glamorous fireplace in the Romantic style. More popular was the late eighteenth-century style known as Etruscan, which manifested itself in graphic red figures against a black background, and found expression in delicately decorated fireplaces bearing the whole array of medallions, masks, palmettes, scrolls, urns and fancy paterae.

Sir John Soane was born in 1753 and died in 1837, at the end of the Regency period in English architecture. He was smitten with the work of Robert Adam, and refined its whimsical neoclassicism into a more severe and rectilinear style, which prefigures the unadorned simplicity of Art Deco and modern minimalist taste.

The Regency period's multiplicity of architectural fantasies and follies, and their undisciplined extravagance, instilled a desire in Soane for 'the unity of the arts'. His London house has exemplary fireplaces of white marble, incised with shallow flutes, minimally decorated with square paterae at the corners, and containing plain rectangular grates. This unrelieved pure geometry lay dormant during the second half of the nineteenth century, but resurfaced triumphantly in the 1930s.

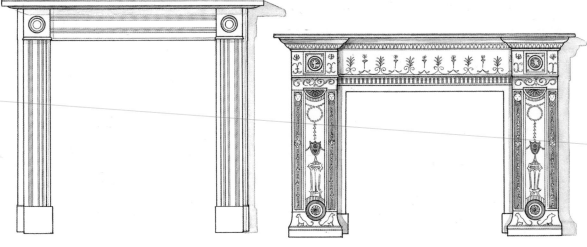

Top left This surround has the reeded jambs and corner roundels that were standard in a Regency design.

Top right The late eighteenth-century fashion for Etruscan motifs on the frieze and jambs was fuelled by archaeological excavations in Greece.

Top left This reproduction pays great homage to John Soane – symmetrical lines and corner paterae are found on both the surround and inset, and Greek figures decorate the rectangular grate.

Top right Beautifully carved scrolls bring a feeling of movement to this basic white marble fireplace in Soane's London house.

Bottom left Elements of this fireplace suggest that it may have been inspired by the designs of James Gibbs.

Bottom right Carved tablets were popular during the first quarter of the nineteenth century.

Bottom left In America, classical Georgian and Regency styles were scaled down to a graceful simplicity.

Bottom right The classical style can be successfully matched with almost anything, such as this Victorian cast-iron surround.

creature comforts

FOR CENTURIES, WARMTH and comfort were minimal and subject to all manner of subversions. Until window glazing became common and carpenters refined the fit of doors, draughts assailed every corner of the room. The classic settle – a narrow seat; straight, high back; and solid wooden underseat – was designed expressly to protect the fireside guest from gusts of cold air. Cushions stuffed with anything from bracken to sheep's wool and horse hair buffered the backside.

With the Georgians, and their serious attention to the niceties of life, furniture became less straight-backed and penitential. In Thomas Chippendale's work, wood cleverly carved in the Gothic or *chinoiserie* style was paramount, and by the time that Thomas Sheraton was in business half a century later, the desire for softness, padding, and silk or chintz covers was being catered for in chairs, couches, beds and chaises longues. By the late eighteenth century, furniture that was light enough to be moved easily was becoming increasingly popular, allowing people to draw their seats closer to the fire if so desired. People began to lounge and relax more as comfort took precedence over formality.

Top left This stylish Georgian fireplace is complemented by original pieces of furniture, including a beautifully upholstered high-backed chair.

Bottom left The opening of this original fireplace has been decreased to allow it to accommodate the log-effect gas fireplace that now warms this attractive period room.

Right A wood reproduction of a Regency fireplace with Victorian inset is joined by a cosy armchair. Towards the end of the Regency period, more luxurious and comfortable furniture began to be produced.

REGENCY FURNITURE

Upholstered furniture was required for reception rooms, to bring a touch of comfort to rooms whose purpose was to relax and entertain. Chairs were often broad, with a deep seat and square back. This would allow room for billowing dresses. The upholstery may have been in tapestry, brocade or cut velvet, and often matched the wall coverings or drapes.

The back of this beechwood fauteuil is slightly reclined into a relaxing position.

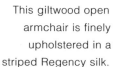

This giltwood open armchair is finely upholstered in a striped Regency silk.

For those craving comfort, this daybed would have been more than satisfying.

chapter 4

From
Colonial
to Federal

This eighteenth-century room would not look out of place in a modern house, with its neat storage solutions and the use of natural materials in an almost minimalist style for both the fire and the surround.

The American Colonial design period began with the courageous founders of Jamestown, Virginia and Plymouth, Massachusetts, and their descendants. Mainly British settlers, they brought with them their habits and expectations for Tudor architecture. Early structures derived largely from English prototypes, but before long intense regionalism developed, and was indicative of the pluralism of American society. One of the most influential documents on the style of this period was James Gibbs's *The Book of Architecture*. Confusingly, American Georgian is also known as Colonial, and it describes an architecture that refers directly to British Georgian style, with an air of the classical. After the Declaration of Independence in 1776, the equivalent of Britain's Regency style was dubbed Federal.

the kitchen fireplace

EXAMPLES OF THE earliest Colonial fireplaces have been painstakingly preserved and restored, and they are inevitably found to be cooking fireplaces. Hefty oak beams still span massive brick hearths in the John Alden House, Duxbury, Massachusetts, the Paul Revere House, Boston, Massachusetts, and Jefferds' Tavern, York, Maine. The brick and paved floors sport a motley selection of cooking equipment, cranes and adjustable spits. Cubbyholes for logs and ovens are neatly incorporated into the brickwork at the side, and bunches of herbs hang drying from the rafters, conjuring up an accurate picture of domestic life. There is a very obvious continuation of the solid, plain Elizabethan country style and, as well as being multifunctional, these fireplaces are definitely the heart of the house. Joseph Alonzo Warren, from Grafton, Massachusetts, describes his childhood experience: 'I will take you back when we were living at home in the large kitchen with the large fireplace, so high and wide that I could stand at the end of the fire in the fireplace and look out of the top of the chimney, and sometimes it would rain in my face.'

For all but the richest, the kitchen was the multipurpose room in which the family ate, worked and relaxed, and, until the eighteenth century it was also the master bedroom. A trestle or folding table would make its appearance at mealtimes, and was then pushed out of the way against a wall so that seating could be rearranged to take advantage of the fire.

Below Spartan comfort in Civil War America – cosy but plain, the high fireplace is dominated by the stove, evidently used for both cooking on and relaxing by.

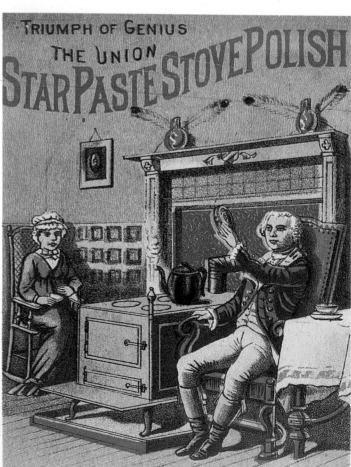

Right Although now used to display antique plates, the mantleshelf would have originally had a practical use – storing essential items that the cook would want to access easily while operating the crane (seen here to the right of the fireplace) or while cooking bread in the back oven.

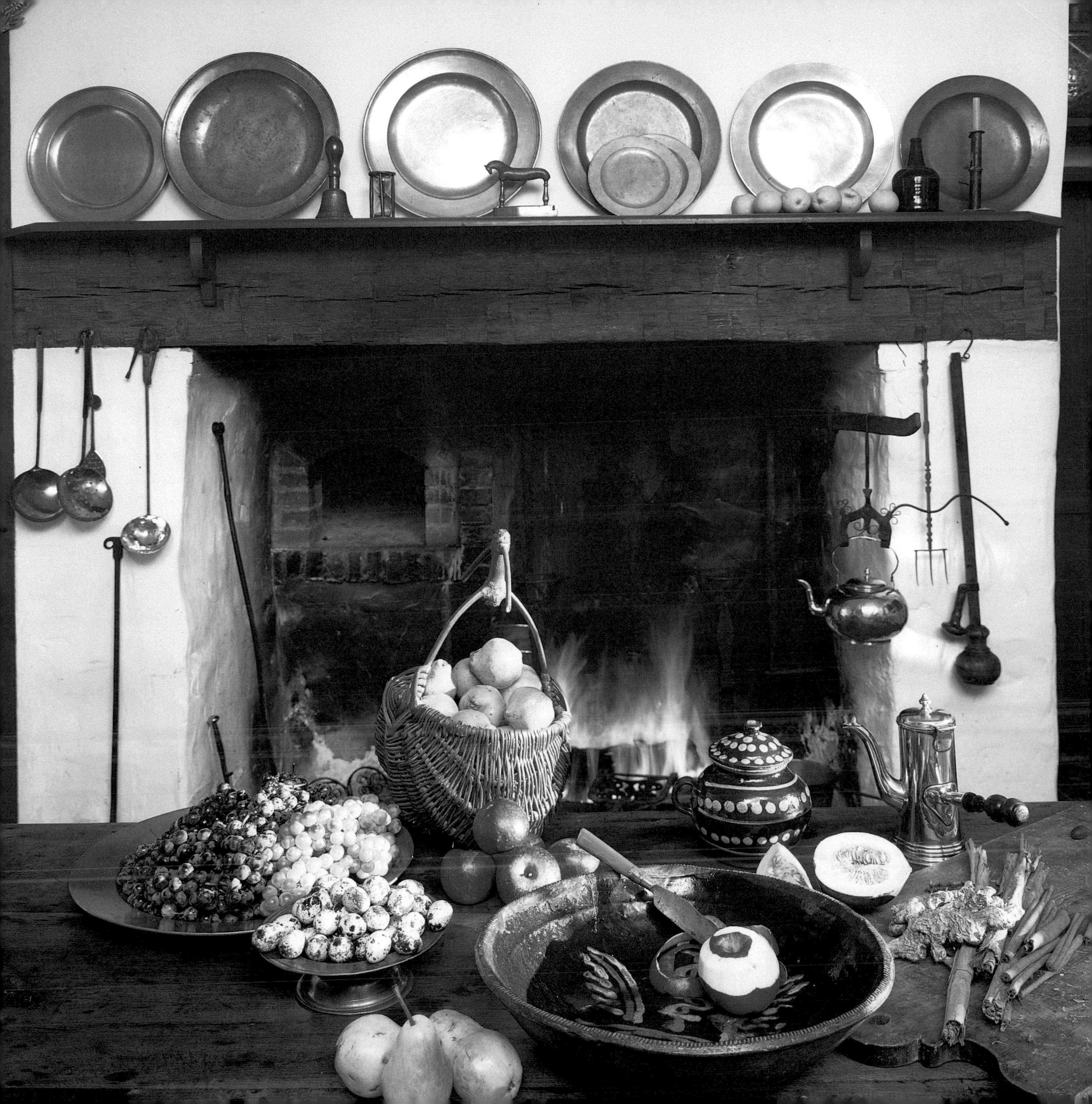

Shaker style

THE NEW ENGLAND Shakers staked their claim to America in 1774. Their brilliantly simple innovations, such as increasing floor space by hanging furniture from the walls, had an original purpose of giving greater space for shaking in honour of God.

Shaker interiors have a bare elemental quality that cuts through the cluttered materialism and ugly artefacts of everyday life. The Shakers' thrifty and utilitarian aesthetic has inadvertently become one of today's great style icons. Their work is the perfect synthesis of beauty and utility, finding contemporary expression in the work of minimalist architects.

The Shakers favour stoves over fireplaces. The tradition is for a plain, low, functional rectangular stove on legs to burn in the centre of the room, with the flue acting as additional central heating. The multipurpose stove serves for warmth and cooking, and the top is used for heating the flatirons that give their textiles a characteristic crispness. Shaker cast-iron stoves are typically just 30 inches wide, with a hinged, lockable door, and an integral semicircular apron at the front. Like everything that the Shakers use, the stoves work with admirable economy and efficiency.

Top left A high-level wooden dado rail serves the practical purpose of hanging items of furniture from, leaving a clear space for shaking.

Bottom left Shaker stoves are traditionally placed in the centre of the room to provide all-round heat.

Right The large apron at the front of Shaker stoves is their most distinctive feature.

a taste for formality

THE INHABITANTS OF the burgeoning towns and cities of the New World wanted something refined and in line with European fashions. A change of attitude was required, as the unbridled felling of mature trees for house building was beginning to denude the native woodland. By the early eighteenth century, the massive and irregular timber frame had been abandoned in favour of brick, and the American house has all the symmetry and gentility that characterises Georgian elegance. Houses began to take on the welcome trappings of civilisation, and fireplaces were placed in bedrooms as well as parlours. Painted cool blue-grey, stone or dark brown to blend with the decor, wood was still a favoured medium for mantles, which had a decorative delicacy, leagues away from the single, dominating multipurpose hearth. They were flanked by architectural pilasters and decorated with a deep frieze and sculptural panels carved with fruit and flower motifs. The mantle was also used to display decorative touches, such as samplers, improving mottoes or mementos.

As people began to prosper and accumulate more possessions, the mantlepiece evolved into something of a showcase. The lip widened and particular adornments appeared, such as shallow painted clocks and ornately framed mirrors. But a certain austerity continued to characterise these interiors, and the simple hearth as a vacant element in a neat geometry of wood panelling, topped with a painting or mirror, remained a favourite well into the 1700s. This look culminated in the 1760s in houses that combined the cool, spacious grandeur of the Georgians with a touch of the monumental, harking back to bold Tudor days, with artfully and expensively grand carved brownstone fire surrounds, set within a regular panelled wood background.

Top left The unassuming wood and tile fireplace was typical of those found in 'middle-class' houses in the mid-eighteenth century. The room is brought to life by the truncated military fire screen, which repeats the style of the portrait above.

Bottom left The fine art of wood-carving was often demonstrated on the fireplaces of the rich in colonial America.

Right This grandiose fireplace sits comfortably among such fine items of furniture, and perfectly demonstrates the desire among the more wealthy New Englanders to emulate the homes of their English contemporaries.

wood surrounds

WOOD FEATURED IN mantelpieces in many different guises. Initially there were simply massive, unadorned rough-hewn timbers, later refined into a soffit board, and eventually a narrow mantlepiece. Above, there might be bare, plastered wall, wooden panels, a painting, a mirror or, if the fireplace was in a corner, cupboards.

As the treatment of the fireplace and its surround became more sophisticated, so too did the treatment of the wood used. At this point, a rich array of paint effects, such as marbling, striping, stippling, vinegar graining, painted landscapes and stencils of varying complexity, were all common adornments. All the finishes that found their way onto wooden furniture also appeared on mantelpieces, or stencils were used on the wall to outline the top surface. The methods of applying paint, and the finishes that they produced, were limited by the tools that could be manufactured at home, yet these often proved surprisingly effective. Turkey feathers, used for reproducing the veins in marble, corks and sponges for mottled effects, a stiff leather comb for wood-graining, and brushes made from cats' fur, were all typical tools.

The interior of a Colonial home was exuberant with colour, as walls, floors, woodwork and exteriors, as well as furniture, would have been painted. Overmantles were frequently decorated with a painted landscape, busy frescoes that depicted farmyards or seascapes, or perhaps the Garden of Eden. In summer, the blackened hole left by the unlit fire would be disguised with a decorative fire screen, which also stopped dust and ash billowing into the room.

Left The wood surround of this fireplace extends to take over the entire room – from mantlepiece to walls and doors. Such extensive use of wood panelling was common in the homes of more wealthy citizens.

COLOURS TO DYE FOR

In the early days of decorating the American home, the colour palette was determined by what could be found in the neighbourhood. Clay made yellow, grey, red, even greenish tones; skunk cabbage, wintergreen, and dogwood produced richer greens; dark pink came from the roots of madder; boiled walnuts yielded mahogany; and boiled chestnuts, red oak and hickory were all subjected to arcane treatments to produce a range of browns. Blue was treated as exotic, since the indigo had to come all the way from India.

Easily grown in the vegetable plot, cabbage produced a lovely, rich green tone.

Madder root was of great commercial importance until the end of the nineteenth century.

Abundant walnuts were among several nuts that were boiled to extract a colour dye.

chapter 5
The Diverse Style of the Victorians

The highly ornate Durbar wing of Osborne House, Queen Victoria and Prince Albert's country retreat on the Isle of Wight, was built by craftsmen from India in 1890–91 to provide more formal State rooms. A carved peacock, a traditional Indian symbol, forms an impressive overmantle.

The Victorians were in the glorious position of having a burgeoning technology, increasing wealth and the chance to pick from every style that had preceded the mid-nineteenth century. They could take a dollop of Regency and mix it with a touch of *chinoiserie*, and add an Egyptian sphinx if desired. There was a sudden explosion of possibilities, and a whole world of plundered styles. Exasperated, one architectural critic wrote;

'Just when the Gothic house was losing its smartness, when its piquancy had proved such a relief to the refined classic, we suddenly found that Queen Anneism was vastly better, and when that had clearly been revivified we found that Dutch and French Renaissance were more interesting; and now, alas! some new prophet asks us to believe in the stiffest of all possible classic...'

Victorian
eclecticism

Right This grandiose cast-iron surround with its unusual, rounded mantleshelf has been stripped back to its bare essentials and joined with a slate hearth to complement the modern touch that this Victorian room has received.

AN INFLUX OF new materials and styles coincided with a building boom. There were many examples of pure pastiche, and many more of a heterogenous medley of whatever took the housebuilders' fancy. Within, this took protean liberties with structure and finish. Consequently, fireplaces from this era might display elements of everything that preceded them as when the Victorians went for ornate there were no restraints. They could and did dive into the past, picking from Louis XIV, Louis XV and Louis XVI, as well as Empire, Tudor, Jacobean, rococo and Adam. Or they might explore the exotic with Moorish, Japanese, Chinese and Indian.

They were also served in this desire for shape and pattern by a repertoire of novelties thrown up by advances in technology, mostly in the areas of moulded fire surrounds, heavily carved cast-iron grates and stoves, and ever-increasing sophistication with faux paint effects.

By the 1860s these amalgamous fireplaces, whether they be neo-Georgian, oriental or neo-Gothic, were normally also covered in an array of objets d'art, such as candlesticks, vases, clocks and other collectible items, and then lavishly decorated with fringed and tasselled pelmets of luxurious fabrics to match the rest of the interior.

Below Victorian sobriety displayed in a sombre partnership of dark marbles and matching hearth. The dark colours are well suited to the classical Regency lines. The fire itself is surprisingly small, and may possibly be part of a later renovation.

COSY CORNERS

The Victorians had an insatiable passion for cosiness, and invented a concept that on rainy winter nights, has a definite appeal. This was the cosy corner, and was the part of a room closest to the fireplace, separated from the rest of the room by insubstantial walls, creating a secluded space just large enough for two armchairs either side of the fire. As well as eliminating draughts, this arrangement brought about a small area of relative calm in the hectic cacophony of a heavily furnished Victorian room.

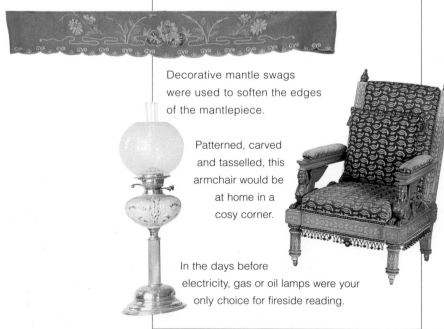

Decorative mantle swags were used to soften the edges of the mantlepiece.

Patterned, carved and tasselled, this armchair would be at home in a cosy corner.

In the days before electricity, gas or oil lamps were your only choice for fireside reading.

ornate design

VICTORIAN INTERIORS MAY have started off simple and classical in design, but, as the nineteenth century progressed, fireplaces followed the popular trend for interiors to be full of colour, detail and texture – the intrinsic virtue of plainness was abandoned.

Few mainstream nineteenth-century homeowners believed in the aphorism 'less is more', and for today's tastes, Victoriana is a synonym for decorative overdrive. The stifling claustrophobia of what constituted a fashionable parlour prior to the twentieth century is well documented – no inch of floor was left unfurnished, no surface was free of ornament.

The fireplace became something of an altar, with overmantles that were shelved, swagged, festooned, mirrored, gilded, putti-decked and trinket-covered. The hearth attracted brass fenders with knobs, fancy grates, brass and iron andirons with twisted obelisks and bun feet, or flaming urn finials. Fire irons had as much extraneous detail as possible without entirely destroying their use, brackets and shelves sprouted from the overmantle, and decorative tiles were used to bring a little extra pattern to fireslips and reveals. Any one detail had charm, but the ensemble jettisoned elegance in favour of excess.

Top left During the Victorian era the mantlepiece became a display cabinet, with additional shelves and alcoves to house treasured possessions.

Top right In this example, the traditional rectangular opening has been heavily ornamented with floral tiles and carved jambs and overmantle.

Bottom left Overmantles were often carved, but tiled ones were more unusual as well as more colourful.

Bottom right Victorians believed that the chimney breast, as the focus of a room, needed much decoration lavished upon it to live up to the scrutiny it came under.

Top left This reproduction fireplace is based on a design that was especially commissioned for the Great Exhibition in 1851, and finely illustrates the Victorian love of embellishment.

Top right Ornate mantle, jambs, hood and fireslips with gleaming fender and fireside tools make this reproduction a perfect example of the Victorian love of mix-and-match decoration.

Bottom left A Georgian fireplace that has been given the Victorian treatment through extensive embellishment and the addition of a fender.

Bottom right Splendid cast-iron Victoriana. This one-piece dark handsome surround with matching hood and fender is embellished with floral motifs on the jambs and frieze as was typical of the period.

the diverse style of the victorians

IF TAKEN TO its bare bones, the Victorian fireplace has a simple elegance that can so often be found taking pride of place in the open spaces and white walls of modern homes. Reproduction Victorian fireplaces are widely available, but if you prefer to go for authenticity, vast numbers of originals can be found in architectural salvage yards, as most nineteenth-century homes had at least one simple cast-iron fireplace with wooden or tiled surrounds. Although it is currently popular to strip the wood and cast iron back to its untouched state, in the nineteenth century, wooden mantles – usually pine – had many different paint finishes, from charmingly naive blotches to tortoiseshell, malachite, marble, stone and dark stains to imitate exotic hardwoods.

simple elegance

Plain, marble fireplaces with a simple brass fender were the order of the day. Ideally, the fender, grate, mantle and overmantle were in the same style, with the fender exactly fitting the hearth. The classic marble fireplace in a Victorian townhouse had, by way of sole adornment, scrolled brackets to support the mantlepiece, or one or two pilasters on each side. This was a graceful distillation of previous styles, perfectly proportioned, and a look that complemented any interior.

Top left An unusual hearth of river pebbles subtly modernises this traditional pine surround with cast-iron insert.

Bottom left A pale marble fireplace from this period easily adapts to contemporary minimalism.

Right This dark marble mantlepiece and stripped-back cast-iron surround would have once graced a dark and sombre Victorian room. Today, it contrasts well against the bright, sunny yellow of the walls and the bold, colourful painting above.

Victorian stoves

Top left This wonderful collection of German tiled stoves dating from 1895 includes stunning examples of a specialised craft. The tiles were often painted and relief-moulded.

CAST IRON BECAME ever more sophisticated as the nineteenth century progressed. Cast-iron grates were made in every style and to suit every need. This practical material was also being used to manufacture stoves in different shapes and sizes, and although the stoves' purpose tended to be decidedly functional, they were often highly embellished. Ironically, today, many homeowners looking for a unique way to warm their living space choose reproduction cast-iron stoves, but often in more utilitarian styles, in keeping with the minimalist look.

In Scandinavia – the country that was at the forefront of stove production and design in the nineteenth century – stoves were objects of beauty. Tiled with transfer-printed Delft or hand-painted tiles, they proudly continued a long Northern European tradition. Stoves were favoured for their economy with fuel, an important issue in freezing temperatures when every room had to be heated. Stoves soon became multipurpose, efficient heating appliances, and were to be found everywhere by the end of the nineteenth century.

Bottom far left This open-range stove with a closed oven for baking was common in the early part of Queen Victoria's reign. The influence of Victorian style penetrated all rooms – a fringed pelmet decorates the mantleshelf, and Queen Victoria's portrait is proudly positioned above the fire.

Bottom left A built-in, cast-iron coal-fuelled range of the type that became the heart of the mid-nineteenth-century kitchen. The Victorians couldn't even bear to leave this functional item unadorned, hence the decorative cast-iron surround.

Top left Cast-iron kitchen ranges and closed stoves were the only source of warmth in a nineteenth-century kitchen.

Top right Victorian stoves can be found in salvage yards and antique shops. It is advisable to get an expert to install them.

Bottom left Carron was one of the largest manufacturers of stoves in nineteenth-century England. This slow-combustion model was particularly popular.

Bottom right This decorative cast-iron stove appeared in a New York manufacturer's catalogue for 1898.

finishing touches

THE VICTORIANS TOOK their passion for decoration right to the heart of the home – the fireplace. The mantles gradually got wider and wider to accommodate ornaments that were spilling over from the sideboards. Fireside tools also received the decorative touch, particularly fire screens. These humble items were given every kind of embellishment besides the more predictable metal mesh, and great ingenuity went into combining frivolity with function. Brass fans were developed that could open from a narrow wedge to a peacock tail, rather like umbrellas, and could be cunningly attached to the grate. Other examples were embroidery protected by glass mounts in hardwood frames, undistinguished works of art in carved and finialled wooden mounts, Islam-inspired fretwork panels, papier-mâché with mother-of-pearl inlay or spray-stencilled with golden ferns.

Pictorial ceramic tiles became extremely popular and were the perfect answer for the Victorian need to make every inch of their surroundings more ornate. Fireplaces were glorious showcases for this art form. The Gothic revival was the catalyst for a passion for tiles, and with characteristic energy, the Victorians explored every decorative possibility and designed them to fit with every fashionable whim. Available individually or in panels, most fireplaces were graced with tiles transfer-printed with animals or flowers. Quaint old-fashioned andirons made a comeback to fit in with the nostalgic architectural theme, the most notable of which were in the form of large brass sunflowers. All in all, firebacks, hoods, slips and surrounds were heavily embellished in various styles, and in order to complement them, all fire accessories, from coal scuttles to fenders, were manufactured in a multitude of designs.

Top left Cast-iron firebacks received the same decorative attention as the frieze and jambs would have done.

Top right As a change from tiles, highly polished cast-iron, steel or brass fireslips with relief designs, such as the classical female figure of Electra, were popular.

Bottom left Floral ceramic tiles were the height of fashion for fireslips in the mid- to late nineteenth century.

Bottom right Classical or romantic figures were often the central design element of long, slim fireslips.

Above The highly decorative moulded brass fire surround is complemented by the brass fender and brass fireside tools.

chapter 6

Return to Individualism

The fireplace in this room is difficult to detect at first, unless you are familiar with the Arts and Crafts style of positioning large fireplaces in luxurious inglenooks. The use of medieval architectural details, as in the Tudor-style four-centred arch that forms the inglenook's opening, was characteristic of the Arts and Crafts movement.

The Victorian era was a time of terrific energy and acquisitiveness. Factories were producing vast quantities of identical items, making them cheaper and readily available to everyone. This in turn resulted in the claustrophobic clutter familiar to us today from paintings and photographs. A counterreaction to contemporary tastes was inevitable. Stifled homeowners fled gratefully to a new generation of homes that had the plain, considered integrity of Arts and Crafts in the work of William Morris or of Frank Lloyd Wright's early houses, or the fresh simplicity of Art Nouveau, as seen in the buildings of Charles Rennie Mackintosh. In contrast to the endless rows of identical Victorian terraced houses put up by speculative builders, these were one-offs, designed to suit the client and a new simplified way of life, but the style they created was easily imitated in existing homes.

Arts and Crafts style

WILLIAM MORRIS WAS the great force behind the nineteenth-century Arts and Crafts movement, and this design trend continued through to the early years of the twentieth century in the work of C. F. A. Voysey, Frank Lloyd Wright and many others. The movement came about as a reaction to the mass-produced ugliness of the dawning machine age. Morris posited 'art made by the people, and for the people, as a happiness to the maker and the user'.

The movement had a significant effect on interior spaces, but as the design reformers who played a role in the movement were all strong-minded individuals, these interiors vary greatly, from minute detail to overall character. However, they all share one fundamental approach – that all items are both useful and beautiful.

Arts and Crafts designs are still easily found in reproduction, and Morris's patterned fabrics have never ceased to be manufactured. This means that it is possible for the contemporary homeowner to aspire to, and achieve, the partnership of beauty and utility that was this movement's hallmark. Natural materials, rich colours and organic designs all produce the comfortable look that is easy to live with.

Top left The unusually high, narrow grate of this fireplace demonstrates the innovative ideas of Arts and Crafts designers.

Top right The exquisite floral motifs featured on fireplaces were often repeated in the wallpaper and furnishing fabrics of the room.

Bottom left The slate surround and subtle geometry of the tiles contrast with the intricate Islamic-inspired fretwork hood.

Bottom right Here, the gentle arch and tiling reveal the influence of Near Eastern designs.

Right This relatively plain stone fireplace with carved stops harks back to the medieval period, while sitting within an inglenook defined by a huge Gothic arch. The large brass and iron andirons and multi-coloured tiles illustrate the eclectic nature that the Arts and Crafts style often took.

Arts and Crafts materials

ARTS AND CRAFTS fireplaces manifested themselves in a wide array of materials. There was solid wood furniture, which ranged from Shaker simplicity to the elaborate, carved whimsicality of Gothic revival, with mantlepieces to match. Philip Webb and Norman Shaw paid obeisance to the Elizabethans with heavy carved stone and herringbone brick fireplaces, adorned with decorative tiles, shapely grates, and brass andirons and hoods. Cast iron was exploited, and entire fireplaces with integral grates were moulded with low relief birds and hearts. The metal fretwork and pointed arches of Islamic architecture made the odd appearance, surrounded by mantlepieces of plain wood with minimal marquetry inlay, or more unusual materials, such as slate.

The medieval look was particularly popular for large rooms that could accommodate such grandiloquence, while it was recognised that more modest rooms were better served by something less elaborate. The fundamental factor unifying these hugely disparate designs, however, was that each would be executed with equal care and attention. The designers of the movement regarded themselves as master craftsmen and only employed master craftsmen. Therefore, whatever the piece – be it a fireplace, chair, lamp, etc. – and whatever the materials used for it, the fine structure and detailing made it a work of art in itself.

Top left The intense patterns and dark colours of William Morris's fabric designs acknowledge the designer's Victorian roots. The fact that they have a timeless beauty is unquestionable, however, as they are still immensely popular today.

Bottom left A plain white wooden mantlepiece with delicately patterned blue and white tiles emits a sense of purity and elegance that would grace any room.

Right Herringbone brickwork forms an extended hearth, and medieval motif tiles form an alternative chimney breast. But to the observer today, the most obvious Arts and Crafts touch is the William Morris soft furnishings.

the style of
Frank Lloyd Wright

FRANK LLOYD WRIGHT changed the look of architecture single-handedly. He took the exterior wood and stucco mainstay of American housing, and gave it a dramatically different feeling, with clean, sharp lines, sweeping horizontal planes and bands of glazing. The inspired use of natural materials – wood, brick and stone – and his benign exploitation of the site are his great legacy to succeeding architects.

Hearths held an innate appeal for Wright, and over seven decades he designed over one thousand different fireplaces. Within his houses Wright swept away all convention, often creating a huge, light space built around a massive central hearth, the ultimate embodiment of both shelter and comfort. The fireplaces were often the anchors of the house, both structurally and aesthetically, while the hearths themselves were cavelike in size and depth, yet always perfectly proportioned for the particular space. The architectural and spiritual importance of a fireplace was innate to Wright, who stated that he loved 'to see the fire burning deep in the masonry of the house itself'.

Top left Stylised geometric motifs are carved into a mantlepiece at Wright's Hollyhock House, Hollywood.

Top right The intricate fretwork in this overmantle was designed to illuminate the natural grain of the oak.

Bottom left A large semicircular arch of tapered Roman brick creates a fireplace of elegant simplicity.

Bottom right The abstract placement of rough-hewn stones forms a sculptural, textural fireplace that can be found in Wright's famous Falling Water house.

Top left This wide, open brick fireplace is very much in the style of Frank Lloyd Wright. The continuous raised hearth provides a useful area for both fuel and personal items.

Top right The crackling fire, handsome fireback, heavy dog basket grate and muted lighting are well framed by the brick surround.

Bottom left Old timber-framed houses may originally have had a stone fireplace, but, influenced by Wright's use of bricks, many homeowners choose to restore their spacious fireplaces using bricks.

Bottom right It would appear from this early fireplace that Wright was heavily influenced by original Prairie houses.

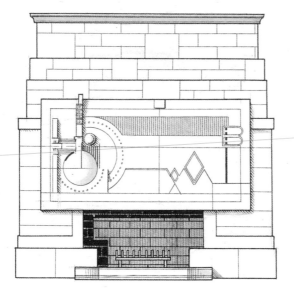

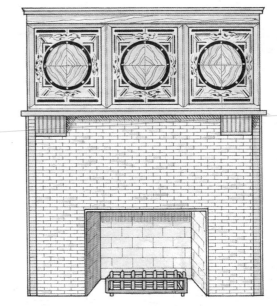

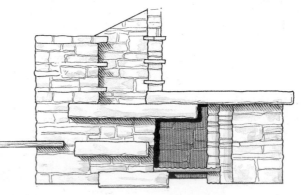

Prairie
materials

FRANK LLOYD WRIGHT sent ripples throughout America with his Prairie houses. Their wide, sheltering eaves and horizontal bands of windows began a trend that still continues today. Perhaps his most imitated strength lay in his original use of natural materials, and stone was one of his most beloved building materials.

Wright was the progenitor of countless rough-hewn interiors, where the fireplace occupies a central, and often structural, role. Mortared stone boulders appear again and again in interiors of the mid-twentieth century, suggesting a ranch house with acres of open grazing land. But this tradition of mortared stone fireplaces – familiar from many a cinematic Western log cabin – goes right back to the earliest native American heritage, and is a technique learnt from the Northwestern Nootka and Tlingit Indians.

Abandoned settlements in the Midwest now consist of nothing more than the stone chimney stacks, the surrounding wooden structure having long rotted away. Country dwellers used what they could find, and rocks were an indispensable part of the building materials. From Mexico to the Yukon, people have piled one rock on top of another, tucked mud in between, and made effective chimneys.

As for aesthetics, everything appears to depend on the integrity with which such a chimney is built. The stone has to be real, irregular, local, and the details, such as timber lintels, have to be in proportion. The stone chimney has a heartwarming nostalgia, a doughty masculine bulk, but is simultaneously timeless.

Above Stone comes in so many varieties that this range alone ensures that it continues to be a popular material for fireplace surrounds. In this example, a particularly light-coloured stone, possibly limestone, was used with a light wood mantle to create a bright and airy room.

Left When houses were built completely from stone, the fireplace and chimney resembled an alcove in a modern home.

Art Nouveau style

LASTING FROM 1890 to 1910, the rich, sinuous, organic style known as Art Nouveau was inspired by Japanese woodblock prints and the Arts and Crafts movement. Originating from these two different sources, it also developed in two very different directions the swirling graphic work of such artists as Aubrey Beardsley, and the spare, controlled geometric designs of Charles Rennie Mackintosh.

Art Nouveau took off like wildfire in France, and the evidence is still visible in the metallic curved entrances to the Metro, designed by Hector Guimard in 1900. Guimard also designed wonderful decorative cast-iron fire surrounds, composed of a concave arch encrusted with elegantly curved stems and blossoms. Others followed suit with ornate plants and animals entwined around the fire, and the copper hood was similarly detailed. Beaten copper, combined metals and marble were used extensively, along with wood, which was painted, stained or artfully veined and streaked to imitate marble.

Top left Turn of the century fireplaces utilised a variety of materials; this one was made from wrought copper.

Top right Relief-moulding was a popular method of imposing the organic shapes of Art Nouveau design onto fireplace surrounds.

Bottom left The distinct Art Nouveau curves that grace this surround were actually carved out of cast iron.

Bottom right This Charles Rennie Mackintosh original features ovals of coloured and mirrored glass set in a mosaic surround.

Top left The cast-iron surround and hood and tiled fireslips all contain the characteristic Art Nouveau shapes.

Top right The elongated curved Art Nouveau forms add a stylish touch to this modern fireplace

Bottom left The style of Charles Rennie Mackintosh betrays a trend toward more austere modernity and the early beginnings of Art Deco.

Bottom right The organic shapes of Art Nouveau spread onto all manner of items, including this stove. Its very curvaceousness makes it look as if it might just start walking about the kitchen.

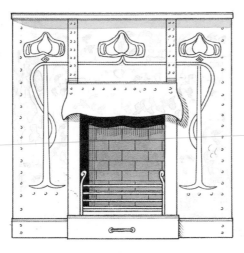

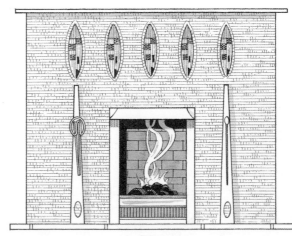

Art Nouveau details

THE SPIRIT OF Art Nouveau found its way onto all the accessories that cluttered the hearth, as well as the fireplace itself. While designers and architects were in their studios thinking of new uses for tiles, the ceramics manufacturer Henry Doulton was busy exploring the practical possibilities. He perfected colored terra cotta and salt-glazed stoneware, creating a warm spectrum from buff through grey to pink and maroon. This stoneware was fired at high temperatures, and consequently fireproofed: perfect for slips down the sides of fireplaces and also for entire mantlepieces, ornately moulded, combining terracotta with glazed tiles. The tile designs could be translated from wood into ceramic, reproduced in quantity, and cast to suit prevailing fashions. Doulton also made economical, miniature smokeless tiled stoves, and manufactured relief-decorated chimney pots.

Elsewhere around the fireplace, stained glass fire screens were produced in abundance, with leaded leaves and flowers held within mahogany frames. Fire irons in steel, gilt and brass suddenly broke into flower, and handles and tongs were entwined with blossom. Fenders lost their rigidity, and took up curves. Firebacks continued the floral theme, and overmantle mirrors positively writhed with their horticultural fruits. If this was all a little excessive, a return to straight lines and simple geometry was forthcoming.

Top left This extremely unusual piece is a ceramic fire cover with an integral grate. Placed in front of the opening it gives a whole new 'face' to the fire, which is still visible through the Art Nouveau-shaped holes.

Bottom left Art Nouveau metalwork was usually of a very high quality, and these intricate fire gates are a fine example of this period's craftsmanship.

Right The popularity of tiles, which really took off during the Arts and Crafts movement, also continued into the age of Art Nouveau. Contemporary designers used tiles as a way of introducing further colour into the interior. Again, motifs that borrowed from nature were the most popular designs.

7

Birth of the Modern Fireplace

The heyday of Art Deco may have been the 1930s, but its instantly recognisable style still holds an allure for lovers of retro, hence the availability of new Art Deco-style fireplaces such as this one.

In the first half of the twentieth century, innovative manufacturing processes and the new demands of a rapidly changing society created a new approach to design, which manifested itself in several different forms: from Arts and Crafts and Art Nouveau came a more industrial look in Modernism and Art Deco.

The Modernist vision of a peaceful machine age, where man could live in harmony with the industrial environment, influenced not only the design of buildings but also their contents. Architects turned their attention to the whole living environment, often making the fireplace the centrepiece of their designs.

early modernism

Right The Arts and Crafts training that Sir Edwin Lutyens received is evident in the fleur de lys hinges on the cupboard doors, but the fireplace is most definitely a move towards modernity.

BRIDGING THE GAP between the Arts and Crafts movement and the early beginnings of modernist movements were architects such as Sir Edwin Lutyens, Le Corbusier and Charles Rennie Mackintosh. Lutyens spanned the Victorian nostalgia for the best of the past with a practicality and simplicity that looked beyond. Although his feet were firmly planted in the Arts and Crafts movement, as were those of Mackintosh, he brought its values triumphantly into the twentieth century. Lutyens's buildings were carefully detailed, with a particular eye to authenticity and affectionate respect for the materials he used. His love of materials was also shared by Le Corbusier, who had a passion for unpretentious and functional materials. Reinforced concrete was typically his proudly flaunted finish. The poetry of his work consisted in the airy floating planes of the structure and the exploitation of the play of daylight within the buildings. Pared-down simplicity, machine-made materials, basic geometric shapes – these are his legacy applied to every detail within and without. Le Corbusier's enduring aesthetic is still manifested today in monumental fireplaces of unadorned slabs of concrete or square hearths plainly tiled.

GUSTAVE STICKLEY

Like Lutyens, Le Corbusier and Mackintosh, furniture designer Gustave Stickley was part of the early modernist movement that bridged the gap between Arts and Crafts and modernism. His solid and elegant pieces often shared the stark angular architectural style of simple squares and rectangles, and rejected all notion of ornament. Such pieces were the perfect accompaniment to the fireplaces of the early modernist designers.

Wood and leather age well, so it's no wonder that this oak chair still looks as appealing as the day it was made.

Stickley's design talents were also applied to lamps, ideal for fireside reading.

Rock yourself into a comfortable doze beside the fire in this wonderfully crafted rocking chair.

Left The repetition of square, angular shapes is made in the armchair and the fireplace. This room, designed by Le Corbusier and P. Jeanneret in 1929–31, illustrates the long-prevailing fashion for clean lines and simple shapes.

Art Deco
colour

ART DECO IS considered to be the first truly international twentieth-century style as it was one that could be adapted to practically any object – buildings, furniture, ceramics, jewellery, lighting – and frequently was. Art Deco was ultimately bold design; if colours were to be bright they had to knock you out, just as if lines were to be clear they should be stark and severe.

Art Deco fireplaces were often striking thanks to the treatment the surfaces received. After the rich, dark colours of Victoriana and the Arts and Crafts movement, design received a revitalising new image with the use of strong, bright colours and clean, fresh pastels. In lavishly decorated items, a variety of colours was often achieved by the use of specific materials, such as inlays of mother-of-pearl or layers of oriental lacquer.

Form, colour, line and volume became important design considerations, and in turn led to the creation of simple shapes and clear, solid colours. Some of the best-preserved examples of Art Deco style are to be found in the cinemas that proliferated across England at this time. The shapes that were used in these buildings reappeared in interior decor, including fireplaces; reproduction fireplaces with radiating, rectangular shapes can still be purchased today.

Above The light yellow marble fireplace is wonderfully complemented by the pale blue marble of the overmantle and blue decoration of the chimney breast. These subtle pastel colours were often used as an attack on the heavy colours of Art Nouveau Liberty designs and the work of William Morris and Co.

Left Lacquered woods and highly polished marble bring warmth and shine to the Art Deco fireplace and furniture.

Art Deco materials

ART DECO WAS an extension of Le Corbusier's 'machine for living in' concept. It was a love affair with the heady perfection of new means and materials – machine finishes, shining tubular chrome, sharp angles, lacquered woods and smooth curves – 'engineer's aesthetic', to quote Le Corbusier again. Art Deco epitomised urban glamour and sleek sophistication. A slick industrial look was aspired to, walls bare and plainly painted, with household paraphernalia becoming as much like machinery as was possible. Electric heaters were almost indistinguishable from car radiator grilles, and the internal workings were no longer discreetly hidden, but proudly proclaimed.

As far as the fireplace was concerned, this spirit manifested itself in billowing, rounded concrete shapes bare of adornment, unless a chrome grille could be accommodated somewhere. Plain, blockish shapes came into vogue too, sometimes covered in tiles or mirror glass. Among these hard surfaces and unyielding geometry, the only touch of softness might come from the rotundities of the three piece suite and the odd curve in the masonry.

Top left The combination of brushed steel with rounded wood creates a classic 1930s fireplace.

Bottom left Heavily veined marble in a range of colours created a unique illusion of texture on certain fireplaces.

Right Brushed steel abounds, with angular shapes contrasting with cinematic curves, in a room that brings Art Deco styling right up to date.

tilemania

TILED FIREPLACES BECAME an obsession from the 1920s to the 1940s, embodying crisp, clean, unsentimental modernity. But fireplaces and tiles have gone together since medieval times. Multicoloured ceramic stoves were made in Germany and the Alps in the thirteenth century, initially consisting of ceramic bowls set into the sides of clay stoves to reflect heat more efficiently. There were passing decorative fashions for tiles in the fifteenth and sixteenth centuries, and from the time when the Dutch first introduced cobalt and white tiles to a colour-hungry world in the early seventeenth century, there has been a tradition of tiled fireplaces.

In the twenties, thirties and forties, however, there was a penchant for strong and unusual colours. Modern tiled fireplaces have a stark graphic simplicity that adapts well to life today, and can match the style statements in the home used by city dwellers to stake their aesthetic ground. If spectacularly decorative, the tiles themselves can be the deserving focal point of a main room. A few tiles set into a plain white plaster fireplace, or a rainbow patchwork of handmade, glazed tiles butted together in the Portuguese style can look stunning.

Right This well-preserved tiled fireplace is a perfect example of the trend that swept through middle-class homes in the mid-twentieth century.

Top left Asymmetrical stepping tiles framed with wood were typical of 1930s fireplaces.

Top right Quirky designs using tiles were a specialty, such as this fireplace embellished with an obtruding corner.

Bottom left This modern reproduction in Art Deco style illustrates the continuing popularity of tiles today.

Bottom right In the 1930s, radiating shapes were very much in vogue. The fact that tiles are easy to cut made them practical.

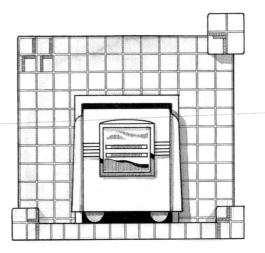

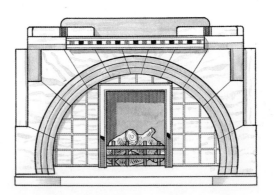

finishing touches

THE MANTLEPIECE CONTINUED to attract decorative items, but in a more subtle and tasteful manner than had been evident in the previous Victorian age. Glass vases were produced in simpler, more geometric designs in the Art Deco period than had been evident through Art Nouveau. By the 1930s, however, a transition to more solid and angular forms was evident, reflecting a change in style that affected all manner of goods.

In ceramics there was a wave of experimentation with form, but, as with glass, by the 1930s the emphasis had shifted. These years saw more simple, restrained forms that were less cluttered and more consistent with interior decor. Heavy patterns were replaced with more solid decoration in pale and muted colours.

A clock continued to be a popular mantlepiece item through the interwar years. Two new materials that proved extremely versatile, bakelite and chromed steel, were often used in such items. Clocks of this period often reflected the industrial moulded shapes that were fashionable for radios, toasters and other gadgets.

Right As long as your fireplace is simple, you can still create a period feel without changing it, simply by adding authentic period furnishings, such as an armchair, lampshade and screen.

Below Highly polished steel in repetitive straight lines, with minimum detailing on the sides, forms this Art Deco grate.

A SHAPE REVOLUTION

More than ever before, the 1920s and 1930s saw designers using metal in product design more and more, enabling a radical change in shape. Angles abounded, in sharp contrast to the sinuous curves of Art Nouveau; the influence of Cubism, which had taken off in the art world, was undeniable. This taste for a sharper look spread to the world of ornaments, making Art Deco an immediately recognisable style.,

The distinct curves of this plush leather armchair are controlled rather than relaxed.

This unique silvered bronze and enamel clock would make a style statement on any mantlepiece.

Chrome for the hectagon base and frosted glass for the jellyfish shade make this lamp a good example of the new materials and shapes.

chapter 8

Contemporary Vernacular

Marble, wood, metal and plaster – this fireplace uses practically every material possible, and in the most unique ways. It is an eclectic mix of different styles, from medieval to Baroque and Art Deco, but is ultimately an utterly individual modern fireplace.

Centuries of trial and error, of tradition, of different solutions, are at our disposal today. We are in the happy position of being able to pick and choose from the best that history and industry have come up with. Tiled or wood surround, plain or ornate overmantle, cast-iron woodburner or gas-fired coal or log effect – there is an embarrassment of riches where fireplaces are concerned. The deciding factors for most people are the style of their room and the demands of their lifestyle. Proportion and period govern the match between the fireplace and its surroundings, while fitting, fuel and finish all have to be considered as well. With all the bewildering choices, having come to a courageous decision, prepare to bask in delicious contentment in front of a roaring fire.

kitchen fireplaces

KITCHEN FIRES ARE comfort itself. They radiate good old-fashioned nostalgia, the image of coming home from the cold outdoors to smell the warming aroma of baking, while children are scattered about a sagging couch and a motley array of dogs slumber on an old rag-rug. This may be the life of times past as we imagine it, and most people do not live like this anymore.

However, an open fire, in what is for many people still the heart of the house, cannot but conjure an image of flickering flames. The idea is romantic, but the reality may not be. Slick urban kitchens, with acres of white tile and chrome, are best served by the work of contemporary designers, with gleaming sculptural shapes that look like jewellery made large; or by the utter simplicity of the waist-high Scandinavian hooded hearths, doubling as barbecues, with convenient niches in which to warm bottles of red wine. Otherwise, choose the constant heat emitted by stoves that stay on all year round and not only allow you to cook food, but warm the room and provide hot water and heating throughout the house.

For those who like to spend most of their time in the kitchen, treating it as the family hub, the kitchen is not usually a room for show, more the magnetic centre of a home. In a working kitchen, butch brick and rough-hewn timber lintels have an appropriate history. If you search around, you can find Edwardian mantles, whose workmanship is often superb. Pitted with shelves and niches in shiny wood, they are excessive in their intended state, but become a friendly presence when stripped and stained, limed or painted, and strewed with juvenile art and crowned with cut fresh flowers in jugs.

Top left Typical English country kitchen style – the gleaming Aga recessed into a tiled nook, but with the added originality of a Tudor four-centred arch as a surround.

Bottom left The great open kitchen fireplace is not unique to times past, and you may well wish to reinstate one to your home if space allows.

Left & above For those who love the modern look – a waist-high fireplace with slats to accommodate a grill, and a hearth shaped into a bowl to keep warm the tasty items just cooked.

living room

THE LIVING ROOM has pretensions. This is where you meet strangers whom you wish to impress, and this is where big and sociable celebrations can occur. This is the place where you will want to make an impression. You can allow a fireplace to make a strong statement, whether your taste is for comfortable, dust-accumulating clutter or imposing monumentality. Coordination is the secret, and everything should work together in symphony.

If retro is your passion, and you just happen to have come across a superlative 1930s smoothly moulded concrete fireplace, you should follow it through with wide, curvaceous furnishings, chrome and glass tables and an expansive, woollen rug with cool swirls. Modern fireplaces are every bit as exacting, if not more so, and you have to be prepared to live up to your heating. Details, such as fuel containers and tools, need careful consideration, and any mismatching just will not do.

Earlier eras are more forgiving of an eclectic mixture, and you can put your grandmother's needlepoint rug with painted secondhand furniture, or bright Italian frosted glass lighting next to a Victorian fireplace. Whatever your era, and however catholic your taste for accessories, the most important factor is to keep within a limited range of colours. Pick out a common denominator of two or three colours to make a sonorous base chord, and then build cautiously upon them. Perfectly matching elements tend to look dead overall, but slight variations on a theme, with an occasional small discord, harmonise and buzz with vitality.

Left A former window has been transformed into a chimney. This perfectly proportioned fire has been custom-made for the flue to take the gas fire fumes straight out of the former window. The rich colours of the velvet sofa and silk cushions give the overall room an Eastern feel.

Top right The basic hole in the wall is ever-popular, this time with the clever addition of a raised hearth to allow space for logs beneath.

Bottom right A scaled-down version of a Frank Lloyd Wright-style brick fireplace, painted white to meld into the overall decor and to emphasise the wonderful greenery of the surroundings.

contemporary vernacular

bedroom
&
bathroom

BEDROOMS AND BATHROOMS are private sanctuaries where you can indulge a softer, less rigorously correct side of yourself, and firelight is a notoriously seductive addition to the atmosphere. This is where gas coals come into their own – a wonderful invention, producing instant heat with none of the labour.

Original upstairs fireplaces tend to be small and delicately detailed, with reeding, roses and integral grates. Cast iron is a typical material, since the great age of the bedroom fireplace was the nineteenth century, when cast iron was the smart new affordable material. Purists keep them shiny black, others paint them white, thereby accentuating any fine detail. There are few experiences more deliciously soothing than taking a bath by candlelight and firelight, and swathing yourself in thick towels that have been warmed by the fire. This is the prescribed antidote to too much work and too little time. The hassle of installing a fire is more than offset by the greedy, sensuous pleasure of having one all to yourself.

Top right This original brick-lined fireplace has been reclaimed by the householders, and transformed into a modern accoutrement by adding a brushed steel surround.

Bottom right Replace the television with a blazing fire. A wide alcove with a polished granite hearth neatly accommodates this perfectly proportioned fireplace.

Left What could be more luxurious than a spacious, yet cosy bathroom in the eaves with the added extra of a blazing log fire? This Victorian fireplace – which would have once warmed a servant's room – has been delicately restored.

ALL THE THOROUGHLY sensible reasons for installing stoves that have made them essential where winters are pitiless still remain. They are clean, tidy, safe, economical, emit lasting heat and look after themselves. Added to this, they look good. Across the western world, stoves have been subjected to every type of decorative finish – tiled, enamel and chrome, terracotta, unassuming cast-iron, and brass. Designed to look like Gothic towers, Greek columns, Roman urns, 'olde worlde' gingerbread cottage ovens and Cadillac grilles, or as crisply engineered as an Apollo spacecraft, stoves can be as quaint or functional as you wish.

stoves

Simplified, stoves are either tall cylinders or smaller potbellies for heating rooms, or horizontal and rectangular for cooking and water heating. Cast-iron stoves were, and still are, the norm, though from the beginning of the twentieth century, curvaceous enamel and chrome in bright colours began to make an appearance. Tempered glass doors mean that the cheering flicker of flames can still brighten a room.

Top left The conical design of this stove provides an excellent view of the fire.

Top right The traditional cast-iron stoves with beautiful tracery on the glass doors were originally woodburning stoves.

Bottom left More and more modern stoves are being made in enamel, as this material enables bold colours to be used as well as funky shapes.

Bottom right This ceramic stove is designed to burn wood or peat, and outside it can burn charcoal without a flue pipe, making it the perfect patio heater.

Top left Sitting comfortably among the paraphernalia of a busy kitchen, this stove will emit a steady, subtle warmth.

Top right A modern take on an old-fashioned style, with a raised hearth that can double as a coffee table.

Bottom left This space-age steel and glass stove allows the fire to be visible from all sides, and is big enough to warm the most spacious of rooms.

Bottom right Ceramic stoves are perfect for those who hate to see a cold, empty hearth. Bright and colourful, they are great to look at, whether lit or unlit.

Top left A Victorian insert and mantlepiece, with the added, unusual feature of engraved fleur de lys to introduce a medieval feel.

Top right The basic hole in the wall goes modern. A simple black-lined hole with safety guard in a stark, white wall to match the interior perfectly. Tradition is briefly referred to with the freestanding marble hearth.

Bottom left The Tudor style can easily be diminished to suit the corner of a modern dwelling. Looked at another way, this is a triple-tiered adobe-style fireplace accommodating logs, fire and ornaments.

Bottom right The classical late Victorian fireplace with fender sits comfortably with Art Nouveau hood and tiles, perfect for those who love tradition but can't decide on a distinctive style.

historical
influences

INTERIORS CAN BE revamped to recreate the feel of practically any era, but even ultramodern interiors often hark back to the simplicity and minimalism of basic hole-in-the-wall fireplaces.

Many people live in buildings that have some history, or even new buildings that base themselves on period style houses. In both these cases there may be an existing period fireplace, a good reproduction or a salvaged piece. If you so wish, it is easy to transform the rest of your room to match the style of your fireplace. The subtle tones of traditional paints can be combined with carefully chosen pieces of furniture in complementary styles to stunning effect. Deep, rich colours are often favoured for period style sitting and dining rooms as they not only reflect the colour schemes of a bygone age, but their bold, dark tones seem to reduce the size of the room; and in the short winter evenings, the light of the fire draws the colours in towards it, creating an intimate space in which to enjoy the company of friends or simply to curl up and read a good classic.

Even if you don't want to go for the period look, you will still find that any fireplace will have some historical associations. The very fact that fire has been around since time immemorial, and that fireplaces have been the central focus of the home for centuries, means that past reference is practically unavoidable, no matter how innovative the design.

fireplace as decoration

Right An unused fire surround can be put to use in the garden or conservatory, creating an unusual yet interesting feature.

THE DECORATIVE POTENTIAL of fireplaces in themselves can be judged by the alacrity with which some Japanese buy them to place against a wall, often beneath a window, simply as sculpture. An empty unlit fireplace is a vacuum that draws attention to itself because of the focal nature of a fireplace in a room. This is where brimming pots of white orchids or coppery hydrangeas, fragrant crates of narcissus, a large and frothy fern, a blaze of sunflowers to mimic flames, broad and bold paper fans, neat pyramids of logs or pine cones, and, naturally, decorative fire screens, come into their own, filling the yawning gap with a touch of colour during the summertime.

As a decorative feature, a fireplace's mantle can be effectively used as a shelf, while its great central gap becomes an attractive niche to fill with flowers, dummy boards, bookshelves, painted cupboard doors, a large ginger cat in its basket, or whatever happens to fit the space and your tastes.

Below What better place to focus your Christmas decorations than along the mantlepiece – candles have always been popular fireplace ornaments, and alongside ivy and fruit create a festive feel.

FIRE SCREENS

Fire screens are widely available: from the antique to the glass-and-brass minimally modern. A carefully fitted fire screen is useful protection against soot and draughts. Traditionally, you would find depictions of fruit and flowers, family members, nautical themes or landscapes. Stencils against a dark background can be used to achieve a bold style, or you could paint a trompe l'oeil folding screen, or even an original work of art. A successful fire screen should have properly finished edges and perfectly fit the space.

A two-dimensional sheep makes an ideal fire screen for a country cottage fireplace.

This lacquered fire screen has an oriental feel to it.

A Pre-Raphaelite image forms the focus for this traditional fire screen, with a finely turned wood surround.

chapter 9

Ultramodern

The perforated metal hood and the steel flue give this fireplace a semi-industrial feel, but the white plaster chimney breast and walls ensure that overall the room has a crisp, clean feel.

There is a reaction to every era and every fashion – country comfort has been a watchword for decades, and is beginning to look predictable to some eyes. Energetic young city dwellers, glorying in the clean, uncluttered expanses of converted factories or airy lofts, have tired of old-fashioned conventions. There is a move towards the spare simplicity whose origins you might find in a Mies van der Rohe or John Pawson building, in a Ben Nicholson sculpture or a Miró painting. The result is a new take on an old theme. Warmth and comfort are taken for granted, but the fireplace is now a material masterwork; the new materials with which it is made turn it into a sculpture, brought to life by leaping flames.

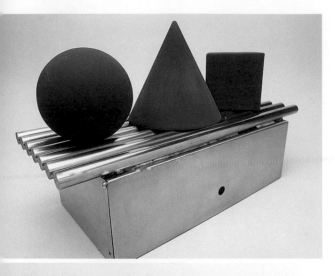

beyond
tradition **AT THIS POINT**

in time and technology, none of the old traditions apply. You do not need to chop down a tree or mine the earth to make fire. Rather it is possible to explore the possibilities of wit and style with modern gas fire 'fuels', or geologs. These come in whimsical shapes and colours – cubes, spheres and pyramids in candy-store pastels – that are there to put the fun into function. They do have a nominal function of dispersing the heat, but their main pretext for sitting fetchingly among the flames is just that they look attractive.

When the fire is alight, gazing into the flames is as happily trance-inducing as it always has been. When the fire is out, there is a colourful still life before your eyes, and when that becomes banal you can just go out and buy different shapes, different colours, for evermore. So, go ahead and give a modern accent to your existing fireplace or create a totally modern setting.

Top left Stainless steel tubes form a grill-like grate upon a utilitarian steel controls box. The matt black geologs will suit those with minimalist tastes.

Middle left This architectural rectangular steel basket has its manual controls concealed behind a cover plate, and is big enough to fit geologs in all shapes, sizes and colours.

Bottom left Bowl-like grates bring a whole new dimension to domestic fires.

Far left
Contemporary
ingenuity. A scalloped
grate embraces the
flames, while an
integral fire screen
frames a unique glass
plate when not in use.

Top left In this
unusual 'firebowl' two
concentric bowls sit
neatly together, the
lower one enabling air
to get to the fuel that
sits in the upper one.

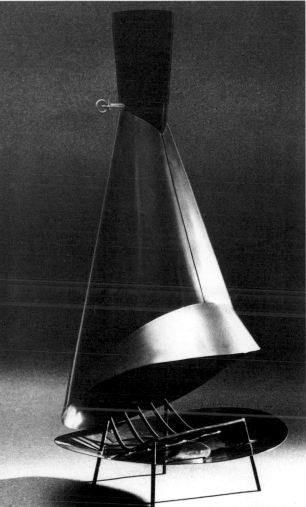

Bottom left A
twentieth-century image
of a twenty-first century
fire. This space-age
design, typical of post-
war innovations, failed
to take off; today
people are often more
adventurous with the
design of their homes,
and new innovations
really are successful.

.new innovations

RADICAL RETHINKING OF all the habits and problems associated with fireplaces has resulted in some clever innovations and startling designs. The materials are unashamedly masculine, without a hint of prettiness or extraneous detail. Metals of various kinds are used, sometimes polished, sometimes roughly textured, whereas concrete is coloured pitch black or virginal white. The fireplace no longer sits quietly on the floor: instead it proclaims itself with an in-your-face brashness at waist or even shoulder height, demanding attention. The fire as source of heat is secondary to the fire as visual tease. Paring down the nonessentials is the impetus. Thus, cunning engineering is used to create an integral grille for safety, which flips out of the way when not needed. The shape of the fire is redesigned completely, and what used to be called the grate is now a neat bowl, in unconscious homage perhaps to the ceramic origins of the European stove. From a hole in the base of this, ashes trickle politely, tidily, away.

These are fireplaces with a brutal beauty, and take some living up to. If your life is perfectly controlled and your habits perfectly clean, then a monument of pristine whiteness with a radiant – literally – work of art at its heart may be the home for you.

location, location, location

IF YOU ARE replacing an existing fireplace or reviving a blocked off chimney, you will have a blueprint for its position and will probably stick to precedent. However, if you are building a new house or considering installing a fireplace from scratch, you have a huge range of options at your disposal. A corner fireplace is cosy for two people. With large, sociable rooms you can be bold and have a central freestanding fireplace or stove – there is an atavistic allure to this, since it sets off distant folk memories of sitting round camp fires. It also means that many people can pleasantly roast themselves.

Alternatively, you can turn to new technology and make use of direct wall venting, convector fires with powered flues that need no chimney, or vent-free fireboxes. These options mean you can have a fire in a peninsula wall, under a window, or installed in the wall between two rooms.

Ultimately, the choice is yours!

Top right A clever use of a fireplace – geometric shapes carved out of white concrete are joined by a line of flames, all positioned at picture height to resemble a work of art.

Bottom right An impressive fire for an impressive room, with an equally impressive view. This freestanding fire with raised chimney enables you to watch the fire burn without having your back to the amazing panorama.

Left For the ultimate in unusual locations, place the fireplace outside! Use it as an ordinary open fireplace to relax by in spring or autumn when the sun is not warm enough, or transform it into a sophisticated barbecue for entertaining in the summer months.

Right Although centrally located with a style very much of its own, this gas fire with its glass brick fireback is also relatively tucked away by the two solid walls built either side of it.

NEW FIREPLACES, FRESH from the minds of young designers, are shapely and refreshingly unfamiliar. They have been completely rethought, and are now more in keeping with sculptures and objets d'art than ash- and dust-ridden grates.

The use of new materials, technology and fuels means that the traditional anatomy of a fireplace can be done away with. As they are no longer an essential part of the home, their shape has become more emotive than functional.

all shapes and sizes

Top left A white concrete bowl, with a small frontal hole for ash deposits, and a stainless steel grille that can be flipped into action, makes one cohesive design statement.

Left Drawing on nature for inspiration, this is an extraordinary and bold redefinition of a fireplace – a textured pod holding in a seed of flame.

IN FRONT OF THE FIRE

To relax fully in front of your fire you need a big, soft rug on which to lie out. To suit the eccentric designs now available for fireplaces you need an equally up-to-date floor piece. Available in stunning colours and bold patterns, rugs are now more like paintings on the floor than ever before.

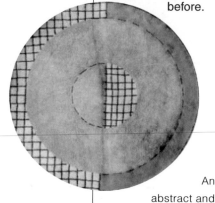

An abstract and humorous pattern brings a sense of fun to your floor.

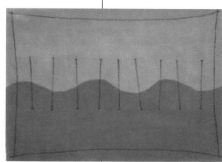

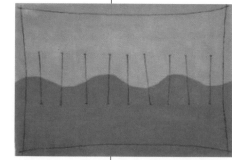

Far right A vast low fireplace with a massive, overhanging canopy is set off perfectly by the equally minimalist and low-lying furniture.

Made from 100 percent New Zealand wool, this rug will be the ultimate in comfort.

modern materials

NOW THAT FIRES and stoves are generally just an agreeable addition to central heating, they do not have to be massive or functional. Instead, unusual materials in abstract sculptural shapes are part of the new fireplace mystique.

Reconstituted stone and plaster are two familiar materials that have been revitalised as they are easily shaped, but more interesting is the use of concrete, glass, bronze and brushed steel. The more familiar marble and cast iron may be found being used alonside these materials, but a touch of the unusual is certainly becoming more and more popular.

Medium-density fireboard (MDF), so long as it is throughly fireproofed, also proves a versatile material to create mantlepieces from – simple to cut and paint, it is perfect for do-it-yourself fireplaces.

Top left Beaten bronze is the perfect material for this unusual 'grate', as it reflects the wonderful flames that fly out of it.

Top right Brushed steel and an exposed flue complement the industrial look of urban loft living.

Top left Talented craftsmen can simulate the finishes of a variety of stone on cheaper materials.

Top right Combine the traditional materials of stone and wood, but choose modern colours such as pure green granite and the lightness of beech to ensure a modern feel.

Bottom left Plain white plaster can't be beaten for simple effectiveness, but add a touch of the unusual with a fireguard in the rich tones of lacquered, rusted steel or coreten.

Bottom right A metallic burnished silver finish adds urban glamour to a room.

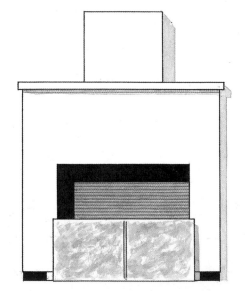

Bottom left Wood itself may not be a new and unusual material in fireplaces, but these rough-hewn blocks of timber resemble logs more than traditional wooden mantles.

Bottom right Fully-fired ceramic 'pots' come in a range of colours and can be custom-made to ensure that they perfectly match the rest of your interior decor.

minimalism

DESIGNERS AND ARCHITECTS have rethought fireplaces and pared them down to an elegant minimum. The point is to maximise the fire and integrate it into the space, while editing out all the distracting paraphernalia. These fires are aided by the use of gas instead of solid fuel – a gas fire does not require log baskets, coal scuttles, pokers and fire tongs.

Minimal, where fires are concerned, is often just a fire and nothing else. Some contemporary designs of a Zen disposition hold the flames seemingly flat on a hearth. Ultimately, this is a very sophisticated return to the original hole in the wall.

It is possible to make your existing fireplace fit the minimalist trend. Remove all but the simplest ornaments from the mantleshelf, paint it the same colour as the walls – preferably this should always be white or off-white – and, if possible, remove the grate, sinking the box to hold the 'coals' into the hearth, so that only the flames are visible. Providing the rest of your room has a similar feel to it – free of clutter and furnished with clean lines and pale colours – you can easily turn a period room into a clean, white space.

Top left A simple square opening with only the slightest hint of decoration in the brass andirons and in the two artistic alcoves for displaying a piece of pottery or tall candlestick, perhaps.

Bottom left A reproduction fireplace that suits the minimalist look. But, were tastes to change, this fireplace could also sit comfortably in a more traditionally decorated room.

Right The minimal ideal – white walls, subtle uplighting, and a fire that gives out a powerful blaze from the polished concrete hearth.

Left Clean, crisp, and white – this beautifully designed bathroom/bedroom/living room is warmed by a real log fire, bringing a touch of nature into a highly stylised space.

urban chic

A CONTEMPORARY INTERIOR need not be compromised by a fireplace. Today, a wide variety of finishes, colours and styles is available, enabling the most image-conscious to find a look that will not be incongruous in their up-to-the-minute home.

Most urban interiors like to use natural, unadulterated materials, and this is where the fireplace comes into its own, with slabs of slate, marble, granite, stone and wood – these can be used individually or mixed and matched. They need little in the way of accessories, as they are more often than not intended to be a style statement in themselves.

Fireplaces in open-plan rooms often introduce a sense of intimacy to an otherwise public setting. Modern sensibilities are appeased by the ease that gas fires offer. If you want a fireplace just for decoration you can just buy a surround and place it against the wall of your choice; there will be no need for a chimney or flue to be fitted, but you will immediately have created a focus in the room.

Above An imposing white overmantle and chimney breast combined makes a strong statement in a minimalist room. The neat space for logs underneath the curved hearth ensures that the space around the fireplace remains free of unsightly clutter.

Resource Directory

AUSTRALIA

Burning Log
40 Cox Avenue
Kingswood, NSW
Tel.: 02-4721-2622
www.nb.au.com/BurningLog

Federation Trading
127 Waymouth Street
Adelaide 5000
Tel.: 08-8212-3400
Fax: 08-8212-1998
www.firstpage.com.au/fedtrading

Gold Coast Fireplace and Barbecue
  Centres Pty. Ltd
94 Bundall Road
Bundall
Tel.: 07-5531-6266

CANADA

The CFM Majestic Products Company
475 Admiral Boulevard
Mississauga
Ontario L5T 2N1
Tel.: 905-670-7777
www.majesticproducts.com

Factory Fireplaces Inc.
15 Grenfell Crescent
Bay 1
Nepean
Orleans K2G 0G3
Tel.: 613-225-7994
Fax: 613-225-7999

Fireplace Direct
33647 Saint Olaf Avenue
Abbotsford
BC, V4X 1T6
Fax: 604-826-0052
www.abbotsford.com/fireplacedirect

UNITED KINGDOM

Acquisitions Fireplaces
24–26 Holmes Road
London NW5 3AB
Tel.: 020 7482 2249
Fax: 020 7482 2949
www.acquisitions.co.uk

Amazing Grates
61-63 High Road
London N2 8AB
Tel.: 020 8883 9590
www.londonfireplaces.co.uk

Anglia Fireplaces and Design
Anglia House
Kendal Court
Cambridge Road
Impington
Cambridge CB4 9YS
Tel.: 01223 234713
Fax: 01223 235116
www.fireplaces.co.uk

Arcadia Stoves
London House
The Green
Shouldham
King's Lynn
Norfolk PE33 0BY
Tel.: 01366 347532
Fax: 01366 347840
E-mail: arcadia@pwnet.co.uk

Architectural Heritage Limited
Taddington Manor
Taddington
Cheltenham GL54 5RY
Tel.: 01386 584414
Fax: 01386 584236
www.architectural-heritage.co.uk

Borders Architectural Antiques
South Road
Wooler
Northumberland NE71 6SN
Tel.: 01668 282475
Fax: 01668 282475
www.salvo.co.uk/dealers/borders

CVO Fire
Studio One
Adelphi House
Hunton
Bedale
North Yorkshire DL8 1LY
Tel.: 01677 450111
Fax: 01677 450937
www.cvo.co.uk

Easy Edinburgh Architectural Salvage
  Yard
Unit 6
Couper Street
Leith
Edinburgh EH6 6HH
Tel.: 0131 554 7077
Fax: 0131 554 3070
www.easy-arch-salv.co.uk

Elgin & Hall
Adelphi House
Hunton
Bedale
North Yorkshire DL8 1LY
Tel.: 01677 450712
www.elgin.co.uk

Farmington Fireplaces
Northleach
Cheltenham GL54 3NZ
Tel.: 0800 7310071
Fax: 01451 860918
www.farmington.co.uk

Kappa Lambda Rugs
Unit 8 Kentish Town Business Park
Regis Road
London NW5 3EW
Tel.: 020 7485 8822
Fax: 020 7485 8866
www.kappa-lambda.co.uk

Lindsay Architectural Antiques
25 Passfield Road
Stechford
Birmingham B33 8EU
Tel.: 0121 789 8295

London Architectural Salvage & Supply
  Co. – LASSCO
St. Michael's Church
Mark Street
London EC2A 4ER
Tel.: 020 7739 0448/9
Fax: 020 7729 6853
www.lassco.co.uk

Marble Hill Fireplaces
70–72 Richmond Road
Twickenham TW1 3BE
Tel.: 020 8892 1488
Fax: 020 8891 6591
www.marblehill.co.uk

Original Club Fenders Limited
Strelley House
Lowdham
Nottinghamshire NG14 7BJ
Fax: 0115 966 5226
www.clubfender.com

Petra Hellas
Unit F1
Toll Bar Business Park
Stackseads
Bacup OL13 0NA
Tel.: 01706 876102
Fax: 01706 876194

Real Flame
80 New Kings Road
London SW6 4LT
Tel.: 020 7736 7906
Fax: 020 7736 4625
www.realflame.co.uk

Rudloe Stoneworks Limited
Lower Rudloe Farm
Box
Wiltshire SN13 0PB
Tel.: 01225 811545
Fax: 01225 811343
www.rudloe-stone.com

Stovax Limited
Falcon Road
Sowton Industrial Estate
Exeter EX2 7LF
Tel.: 01392 474000
Fax: 01392 219932

USA

21st Century Fireplaces
35 Oak Hill
Paradise, PA 17562
Tel.: 717-687-7221
Fax: 717-687-7219

American Stove
5891 Firestone Drive
Syracuse, NY 13206
Tel.: 315-433-0038

Antique Stove Association
2617 Riverside Drive
Houston, TX
Tel.: 713-528-2990
Fax: 713-526-2122
www.antiquestoveassoc.org

Antique Woods & Colonial Restorations,
1273 Reading Ave.
Boyertown, PA
Tel.: 610-367-8193
Fax: 610-367-6911
www.vintagewoods.com

Architectural Accents
2711 Piedmont Road
Atlanta, GA
Tel.: 404-266-8700
Fax: 404-266-0074
E-mail: archaccent@aol.com

Architectural Antiques Exchange
715 N. Second St.
Philadelphia, PA
Tel.: 215-922-3669
Fax: 215-922-3680
E-mail: aaexchange@aol.com

Architectural Artifacts, Inc.
4325 No. Ravenswood
Chicago, IL
Tel.: 773-348-0622
Fax: 773-348-6118
www.archartifacts.com

Architectural Salvage Warehouse
212 Battery Street
Burlington, VT
Tel.: 802-658-5011
Fax: 802-658-5011
www.architecturalsalvagevt.com

Artefact Architectural Antiques
790 Edison Furlong Road
Box 495
Furlong, PA
Tel.: 215-794-8790
Fax: 215-794-7249
www.artefactantiques.com

California Fireplaces
127 N. Magnolia
El Cajan, CA 92020
Tel.: 619-590-0156
Fax: 619-590-0205

Central Fireplace
5525 Transit Road
Williamsville, NY 14221
Tel.: 716-696-9753

Elgin Majestic
824 East Chicago Street
Elgin, IL 60120
Tel.: 847-711-5903

Eureka Stove & Fireside
331 7th Street
Eureka, CA 95501
Tel.: 707-444-2363
Fax: 707-444-3052

The Fireplace
1139 International Blvd
Oakland, CA 94606
Tel.: 800-843-3473
Fax: 510-834-9250

The Fireplace Company
774 Highway 133
Carbondale, CO 81623
Tel.: 970-963-3598

Fireplace Connection
140 26th Street N.W.
Owatonna, MN 55060
Tel.: 507-444-0067
Fax: 507-444-9707

Fireplace Corner, Inc.
2700 Fairview Ave.
Roseville, MN 55113
Tel.: 612-633-1042
Toll-free: 800-541-5411

Fireplace North
121 Kent Street
Iron Mountain, MI 49801
Tel.: 906-774-20211
Toll-free: 800-974-2021

Fireplaces Plus
1133-C 2nd Street
Encinitas, CA 92624
Tel.: 760-436-5343

Fireplace Professionals
1217 W. 41st Street
Sioux Falls, SD 57105
Tel.: 605-339-0775
Toll-free: 800-366-4328

Fireplace Solutions
P.O. Box 610
1208 Tenside Road
Louisville, Tenn. 37777-5505
Tel.: 423-978-0050
Fax: 423 970-2121

Focal Point Architectural Products, Inc.
P.O. Box 93327
Atlanta, GA 30377-0327
Toll-free: 800-662-5550
Tel.: 404-351-0820
Fax: 800-352-9049
www.focalpointap.com

Golden Movement Emporium
5335 West 102nd Street
Los Angeles, CA
Toll-free: 800-590-3288
Tel.: 310-645-3386
Fax: 310-645-8902
www.goldenmovement.com

Good Time Stove Co.
Route 112, P.O. Box 306
Goshen, MA
Tel.: 413-268-3677
Fax: 413-268-9284
www.goodtimestove.com

Historic Albany Foundation and
   Architectural Parts Warehouse
89 Lexington Avenue
Albany, NY 12206
Tel.: 518-465-0876
www.historic-albany.org

Homestead Stove Co.
2729 N.E. Broadway
Portland, OR 97232
Tel.: 503-282-3615
Fax: 503-282-0520

House of Fireplaces
7226 East 87th Street
Indianapolis, IN 46256
Tel.: 317-577-0400
Fax: 317-577-7980
www.house-of-fireplaces.com

Jotul North America Inc.
400 Riverside Street
P.O. Box 1157
Portland
Maine 04104
www.hearth.com/jotul

Macy's Texas Stove works
5515 Almeda Road
Houston, TX
Tel.: 713-521-0934
Fax: 713-521-0889
www.macystexasstoveworks.com

Majestic Mantel
1015 E. Burnside Street
Portland, OR 97214
Tel.: 503-231-7282
Fax: 503-236-6880
www.majesticmantel.com

Malm Fireplaces
368 Yolanda Avenue
Santa Rosa
CA 95404
Tel.: 707-523-7755
Toll-free: 800-535-8955
Fax: 707-571-8036
www.malmfireplaces.com

Mantels of Yesteryear
P.O. Box 908
McCaysille, GA
Tel.: 706-492-5534
Fax: 706-492-3758
www.mantelsofyesteryear.com

Okell's Fireplace
1300 17th Street
San Francisco, CA 94107
Tel.: 415-626-1110
Fax: 415-626-5512

Olde Goode Things
124 West 24th Street
Manhattan, NY
Tel.: 212-989-8401
Toll-free: 888-551-7333
www.oldegoodethings.com

On Fire
3450-G Airway Drive
Santa Rosa
CA 95403
Tel.: 707-526-3322
Fax: 707-526-7963

Preservation Hall Architectural
55 N. Main Street
P.O. Box 977
Weaverville, NC
Tel.: 828-645-1047
Fax: 828-645-1047
www.preservation-hall.com

Readybuilt Products Company
1701 McHenry Street
Baltimore, MD 21223
Tel.: 410-233-5833
Fax: 410-566-7170
www.readybuilt.com

River City Stoves
612 Estudillo Street
Martinez, CA 94553
Tel.: 925-228-5171
Fax: 925-228-5171

Salvage One
1524 S. Sangamon Street
Chicago, IL
Tel.: 312-733-0098
Fax: 312-733-6829
www.salvageone.com

Southern Accents Architectural Antiques
308 Second Ave. S.E.
Cullman
Alabama 35055
Tel.: 256-737-0554
www.antiques-architectural.com

Stoves Direct
Distribution and Sales Office
80 East Wilbur Avenue
Dalton Gardens, ID 83815
Toll-free: 800-395-9509
www.stovesdirect.com

Sutter Home & Hearth
5333 Ballard Avenue N.W.
Seattle, WA 98107
Tel.: 206-783-9115
Fax: 206-784-7569

Teton Fireplace Design
903 East 9400 South
Sandy, Utah 84094
Tel.: 801-297-8500
Toll-free: 888-297-8500

Tony's Architectural Salvage
123 N. Olive Street
Orange, CA
Tel.: 714-538-1900
Fax: 714-538-1966

Western Fireplace Supply
1315 Ford Street
Colorado Springs, CO 80915
Tel.: 719-591-0020

Wilkening Fireplace Company
9608 State 371 N.W.
Walker, MN 56484
Toll-free: 800-367-7976
Fax (toll-free): 800-591-5884
E-mail: wilkenfp@eot.com

Woodstove & Fireplaces Unlimited
193 E. Grove Street
Middleboro, MA 02346
Tel. 508-997-8835

Index

Credits

Quarto would like to thank and acknowledge the following for supplying pictures reproduced in this book.

Picture Research by Image Select International.

b = bottom, t = top, c = centre, l = left, r = right

Abode UK: p38; p97; p105bl; p106; p109tl; p110t & b; p121; p136ct. **Acquisitions**: p37bl; p62bl & r; p63b, c, & t; p73tl; p75; p82b; p91tr&br; p94br; p96tl, bl, & r; p111l, cl, cr, & r; p122bl; p134tl; p134br. **Aisa**: p17tr. **AKG**: p16bl; p19bl; p20b. **J. Allan Cash**: p52tl; p94bl; p105tl; p126b; p134bl. **Amazing Grates**: p73br; p91tl. **Anglia Fireplaces and Design**: p43t. **Ann Ronan Picture Library**: p12t & b; p15; p16t; p7l; p34; p39; p48t & b; p78; p94t. **Arcaid**: p9 (Alan Weintraub); p32/33 (Earl Carter/Belle/Designer: Shane Chandler); p81 (Richard Bryant); p105br (Lucinda Lambton); p123 (Alan Weintraub); p141 (Richard Bryant); p152 (John Edward Linden). **Arcadia Stoves**: p37br; p133br;(Andrew Orr Photographic). **Arcblue**: p49 (Peter Durant/arcblue.com). **Architectural Association**: p14bl; p51t; p51b(Busby, W&H); p52bl (Etienne Clement); p 54bl (Deb Galwey); p71bl (Valerie Bennett); p73tr (Valerie Bennett); p109bl (Hugo Hinsley); p114bl (Carol Shields); p115 (Lewis Gasson). **Architectural Heritage**: p17bl; p40t. **Chris Fairclough Colour Library**: p25. **Christie's Images Ltd**: p74tr, cr, & br; p88br; p114br, c, & t; p122l. **Corbis Images**: p22/23; p24t; p27b (Buddy

Mays); p136bc (Philadelphia Museum of Art, Penn., U.S.A.). **CVO Fire**: p40b; p127l & r; p140b; p142 (all images); p143t; p145tr; p148tl & bl; (All taken by Kevin Radcliffe). **Elgin and Hall**: p136. **English Heritage**: p86. **Farmington Fireplaces**: p133tr; p136bl. **Hulton Getty**: p7r; p41t; p143b. **Interior Archive**: p35; p37tr (Ken Hayden, Designer: Jonathan Reed); p55br; p60t (Tim Goffe); p67 (Simon Upton); p68 (Simon Upton); p69t (Simon Brown); p74tl (Simon Upton, Stylist: Diane Berger); p80t (Fritz von der Schulenburg); p80b (Fritz von der Schulenburg); p82 (Fritz von der Schulenburg, Antique Dealer; John Russell); p89 (Simon Upton); p.92tl (Henry Wilson); p107 (Fritz von der Schulenburg, Florist: Barry Ferguson); p108br (Fritz von der Schulenburg); p116 (Fritz von der Schulenburg); p117 (Fritz von der Schulenburg); p119 (Henry Wilson); p124 (Fritz von der Schulenburg); p128 (Fritz von der Schulenburg); p129t (Simon Upton, Designer: Bill Amberg); p130 (Fritz von der Schulenburg);p131t (Ken Hayden, Designer: Jonathan Reed); p131b (Fernando Bengoechea); p133tl (Fritz von der Schulenburg, Designer: Richard Muddit); p134tr (Simon Brown, Designer: Frank Salkin); p138 (Simon Brown); p144 (Fernando Bengoechea); p145l (Fritz von der Schulenburg); p147 (Fernando Bengoechea); p150t (Edina van der Wyck); p150b (Simon Upton); p151 (Tim Beddow). **IPC Syndication**: p6 (Essentials, Ideas); p10 (Simon Upton, Country Homes & Interiors);

p21 (D. Britlain, Ideal Home); p29tl; p36. **Jessica Strang**: p8b; p24b; p30t&b. **Kappa Lambda Rugs**: p146tc, bc, & l. **Malm Firelpaces**: p145br; p133bl (Austroflamm). **Marble Hill Fireplaces**: p14tl; p62tr. **National Trust Photographic Library**: p45 (Andreas von Einsiedel); p52br & bc (Nick Meers), tr (Andreas von Einsiedel); p70 (Nadia MacKenzie); p71tl (Bill Batten); p71r (Nadia MacKenzie); p88bc (Andreas von Einsiedel); p98 (Andreas von Einsiedel); p101(Andreas von Einsiedel); p102b (Andreas von Einsiedel). **Original Architectural Antiques Co. Ltd.**: p41br. **Original Club Fenders**: p62tl; p91bl. **Paul Rocheleau**: p8t; p31; p46; p53; p56; p57; p64; p73bl; p76; p79; p83; p84; **Petra Hellas**: p109tr; p112. **Phillips International Auctioneers and Valuers**: p122ct & cb. **Pictures Colour Library**: p29br; p43b; p61; p69b; p74bl; p105tr. **Platonic Fireplace Company**: p140t & c. **Powerstock Zefa**: p29tr. **PWA International**: p42. **Robert Opie**: p14lc. **Rudloe Stoneworks**: p55tl & tr; p126t; p41bl. **Salzburger Burgen and Schlosser Betriebsfuhrung**: p29bl. **Scala**: p14r; p19tr; p20t; p26; p27t; p50; p58; p60b. **Spectrum**: p13; p88bl; p129b; p153. **Stovax**: p37tl. **Syon Park Ltd.**: p18. **Werner Forman**: p136r. **Woodmansterne**: p102t; p103.

All other photographs and illustrations are the copyright of Quarto Publishing plc. While every effort has been made to credit contributors, Quarto would like to apologize should there have been any omissions or errors.